EUROPE'S FULL CIRCLE

CORPORATE ELITES AND THE NEW FASCISM

RODNEY ATKINSON

DEDICATION

I dedicate this book to my mother,
Ella May Atkinson, who suggested the title
and to my late father Eric Atkinson MA (Oxon)
who gave me my interest in political economy
and the German language.

Published by

Compuprint Publishing
1 Sands Road
Swalwell
Newcastle upon Tyne
NE16 3DJ

Second revised and expanded edition February 1997

Third revised and expanded edition December 1998

Paperback £10.00 ISBN 0 9525110 3 7

This book is available direct from the publisher at the above address for £11.00 including postage and packing.

Printed by C. P. Print Limited
Newcastle upon Tyne

British Library Cataloguing in Publication Data.

A Catalogue record for this book is available from the British Library

They have given us into the hands of new unhappy Lords
Lords without anger and honour who dare not carry their
swords
They fight by shuffling papers; they have bright dead alien
eyes
They look at our labour and laughter as a tired man looks at
flies
And the load of their loveless pity is worse than the ancient
wrongs
Their doors are shut in the evening; and they know no songs

We hear men speaking for us of new laws strong and sweet
Yet is there no man speaketh as we speak in the street
Smile at us, pay us, pass us. But do not quite forget
For we are the people of England and we have not spoken yet

G.K. Chesterton, *The Secret People*

"The French and Italian statesmen seemed interested in the prospect of the encirclement of England on all seas and all countries facing her shores which, they were assured, would lead to British collapse if the community of which the Fuehrer had spoken was achieved."

Gordon A. Craig, *Germany 1866-1945*, Oxford. 1978, page 725.

For some years past Nordic meetings had been arranged in Germany to which large numbers of Norwegians had been invited. German lecturers, actors, singers and men of science had visited Norway in the promotion of common culture. All this had been woven into the texture of the military plan and a widely-scattered internal pro-German conspiracy set on foot... every member of the diplomatic or consular service, every purchasing agency played its part... The president of the Norwegian Parliament, Carl Hambro, has written:

> "In the case of Norway the Germans under the mask of friendship tried to extinguish the nation....What stupefied the Norwegians more than the aggression itself was the national realisation that a great power, for years professing its friendship, suddenly appeared a deadly enemy and that men and women with whom one had had intimate business or professional relations who had been cordially welcomed in one's home, were spies and agents of destruction... elaborating the most detailed plans for the invasion and subsequent enslaving of their country."

The King, the Government, the Army and the people, as soon as they realised what was happening flamed into furious anger. But it was too late.

Winston Churchill, *The History of the Second World War*,
Volume 1, page 546.

ACKNOWLEDGEMENTS

The author would like to express his thanks to Peter Johnston whose proof reading, advice and contributions to research have been invaluable, to Norris McWhirter and Sir Louis Le Bailly for the benefit of their wisdom and experience in the defence of our nation, Derek Tozer, Michael Champness, Dr Gerard Aalders (Netherlands), Erik Göthe (Sweden), Peter Watson and Leolin Price QC for their contributions of research material or comments on drafts of the book. I am also grateful to many in both Houses of Parliament for their help and support: in particular Sir Richard Body MP and his fellow "Eurosceptics" in the Commons and the valiant Lord Stoddart of Swindon who despite the unprincipled attempts by political parties to suppress their dissent, consistently exposed and rejected the appeasement of their country's adversaries.

CONTENTS

"Just imagine that these events (the extermination camps) were to become known to the enemy and were being exploited by them. In all probability such propaganda would be ineffective because those hearing and reading it would not be prepared to believe it."

Letter from "The Reichskommissar for the Ostland" to the "Reichsminister for the occupied Eastern Territories", 18th June 1943 in *The Yellow Star* by Gerhard Schoenberner, Corgi Edition 1969, p. 97.

AUTHOR'S PREFACE TO THE THIRD EDITION

The third edition of *Europe's Full Circle* two years after first publication is due to high demand for a highly praised product - despite not a single review appearing in any major British newspaper or periodical.

This will come as no surprise to those who have grown accustomed to the longstanding media censorship of the facts about the "European" Union, its destruction of our 800 year old constitution and the attempts by the leading politicians of all political parties to quash discussion of this scandal.

In this third edition a number of additions have been made, the most extensive being in the by now well known chapter 11, in which additional parallels are drawn between the words and actions of fascist Europe of the 1930s and 1940s and the European Union of the 1980s and 1990s. In particular the parallels between the activities of Germany in Yugoslavia and Kosovo today and the attempts by Nazi Germany to undermine Yugoslavia in the 1930s and their break up of that country into many racial and ethnic statelets in the 1940s are of great concern.

Of even greater concern are the parallels between Nazi propaganda methods of the 1930s and 1940s and the attitudes and tactics of the European Commission and the Labour Government today as they manipulate an electorate deliberately starved of democratic knowledge and even of the right to vote on the never ending absurdities of the new Eurostate.

In the introduction further material showing how American companies supported the Nazi war machine makes today's accusations against Switzerland tame by comparison.

The chapter on Bilderberg contains additional material on some of the major supporters of that corporatist and secretive group over the years. In particular a former CIA operative confirms that Bilderberg was by far the most successful promoter of the European Union and the destruction of the sovereign democratic nations of free Europe.

AUTHOR'S PREFACE TO THE SECOND EDITION

Three months after the first print run of *Europe's Full Circle* sales have exceeded supply. It was thought better to produce a new edition, first to make minor corrections, secondly to add one or two explanatory footnotes and third, and most important, to add a new chapter on "The Power of the Nazi Legacy". This new chapter (11) demonstrates, I hope, the extreme danger of the present situation in Europe and how exact are the parallels between the 1990s and the 1930s.

Once again (as in the 1930s, when so few saw the dangers) prescience risks the cries of "Germanophobe" and "anti-German". Once again it must be emphasised that the dangerous political activities of the German government have their avid supporters among the corporatist and quasi fascist forces in other European Union countries, in the USA and even in the United Kingdom. But although democratic forces within Germany are stronger today than in the 1930s, German industry and supranational corporatism are also stronger. The German parliamentary system is young, only 50% of MPs are directly elected and proportional representation leads to covert deal making for the patronage of parties with as little as 5% of the vote.

Italy has averaged more than one government per year since 1945, Spain, Greece and Portugal were relatively recent military dictatorships, the Netherlands provided Hitler with two purely Dutch SS divisions, Belgium is split, rocked by judicial, political and financial scandals and its Prime Minister (the German protegé Dehaene) has suspended democratic rights. France's centralist and dictatorial bureaucracy so alienates its people that "debate" takes the form of street violence, barricades and attacks on foreigners.

The tragedy for the United Kingdom is that on this side of the Channel we seem to have reproduced, man for man, the kind of appeasing, incomprehending and complacent political leadership which led our country to disaster a generation ago.

THE AUTHOR

Rodney Atkinson BA MSc MIL studied at the Universities of Durham and Newcastle upon Tyne before becoming, for 6 years, a lecturer at the University of Mainz in Germany. He returned to take up posts in merchant banking in the City of London before starting his own businesses in property, conferences and publishing. He is a writer on political economy of national and international repute and has been an occasional adviser to Government ministers. He has had articles published in *The Daily Telegraph*, *The Guardian*, *The Times*, *The Financial Times* and *The Wall Street Journal*. He is the author of some 60 articles and policy papers as well as six books - *Government Against The People* (1986), *The Emancipated Society* (1988), *The Failure of the State* (1989), *Conservatism in Danger* (1991), *Your Country Your Democracy* (1989) and, with Norris McWhirter, *Treason at Maastricht - The Destruction of the Nation State* (second edition 1995). He has been a frequent commentator on political and economic affairs on television and radio.

THE AUTHOR'S TRACK RECORD

In this book the author warns of the consequences of economic and political decisions taken by the British parliament and government. If these warnings are to have the desired effect - the reversal of those decisions - then the past record of the author is significant in assessing the credibility of these warnings.

For many years Rodney Atkinson has been warning government ministers about policies which he believed would have disastrous effects. He has also frequently provided analyses which have led to government implementing highly successful policies.

In 1981 in a Bow Group paper "Making Monetarism Work" Atkinson warned that the effect of tight monetary policy on the banks meant that very large windfall profits were being made which in turn led to the expansion of bank reserves and even greater inflation. Not long afterwards a "windfall profits tax" was introduced.

In 1984 the *Financial Times Energy Economist* published the author's article which predicted that oil prices were going to fall significantly. They did.

Throughout the 1980s the author warned of what he termed "Regional Equity Loss" whereby central government taxed companies and individuals in the poorer regions and then put about 95% of every pound back "into the region" in the form of grants and subsidies to foreign corporations producing in competition with British companies. He pointed out that despite billions of pounds having being poured into the North East of England since the 1930s, the region still remained the poorest in Britain.

In 1985 he wrote a Bow Group paper recommending that British Gas should not be allowed (as a monopoly British buyer) to import gas from Norway's Sleipner field since this gas was more expensive than that from British gas fields and was preventing the exploitation of those UK offshore fields. As a direct result of that paper the House of Commons Select Committee held an inquiry and the import was stopped, thus saving the British balance of payments circa £10,000m.

In 1990, four days after the government took the United Kingdom into the European Exchange Rate Mechanism, Atkinson's letter in *The Times* predicted its failure and pointed out that the decision to join contradicted all traditional Conservative economic and political ideals. He also predicted that fixing the Pound exchange rate against the ERM would allow Germany to acquire business assets without any apparent risk of devaluation. He was proved correct, especially as regards German purchase of London property, merchant banks and industrial companies.

In 1991 he predicted in a Bow Group paper *"Mortgage Interest Relief - Time for abolition"* that house prices would fall dramatically. Much criticised by estate agents and building societies, he was proved correct. As he recommended, Mortgage Interest Relief has since been radically reduced, thus saving the Exchequer many billions of pounds per annum.

In 1992 his paper "Real Interest" warned that taxing interest income without allowing for inflation was destroying the capital of savers and distorting capital, housing and government income. The author warned several Treasury ministers and advisers that it was typically Conservatives who were being affected by this policy. In the budget of 1995 the Chancellor of the Exchequer introduced a special 20% tax rate on interest income (but only for basic rate tax payers), which, although an inadequate response, at least acknowledged the problem.

In the early 1990s Atkinson wrote on several occasions to Treasury Ministers warning that their policy of fighting the **symptoms** of inflation (through for example the European Exchange Rate Mechanism) rather than the causes would destroy the Conservative classes and make the socialist classes richer. In July 1992 he wrote to Chancellor Norman Lamont:

> "Government, having failed to tackle both State and corporate collectivism cannot then afford to defeat inflation. The battle will only wipe out the responsible small company, individual saver, non unionised worker, retired middle class and all the other typical Conservatives"

In March 1994 he warned Chief Secretary to the Treasury Michael Portillo of the:

> "... catastrophic consequences for the Conservative Party of exerting strong monetary control while doing nothing to remove the institutional distortions which cause inflation".

Several years later these predictions have come true. The Conservatives' traditional lead over Labour in the social categories ABC1 has been turned into a substantial Labour lead. In April 1996 statistics published showed that there was a higher percentage of Labour voters earning over £20,000 per annum than Conservative voters. Between 1980 and 1990 UK business failures averaged about 15,000 per annum. Between 1990 and 1995 they averaged about 46,000 per annum. In 1990 home owners with "negative equity" numbered 90,000 but by 1995 this had risen to 1.1 million.

Having destroyed the finances of Conservatives it was therefore not surprising that Government policies led to the decimation of Conservative Party finances.

This political and economic failure was paralleled by (and to a large extent caused by) the ultimate failure of any government - the destruction of the British constitution, which the author described in *Your Country Your Democracy - the threat from the European Union* and, with Norris McWhirter, in *Treason at Maastricht*.

INTRODUCTION

By combining the most authoritarian elements of socialism and capitalism under the principles of corporate and State power, fascism succeeds in uniting "left", "right" and "centre". Fascism is not another element in the panoply of democratic choice and freedoms, it is a denial of that choice and a contradiction of those freedoms *and is in part a major feature of the policies of established democratic political parties.*

Since the political state began its inexorable rise at the beginning of the 20th century, the powers accumulated in the name of social concern, business organisation and political rights have become the standard tools of all political parties and have been gratefully accepted and utilised by fascist, communist and even religious dictatorships. As a result those "democratic" parties which claim they are fighting such regimes continue to evolve the political preconditions for those very regimes.

The principal element of fascist systems is not a loud-mouthed dictator but a system of corporate and collective power. Corporations, institutions and collectives, backed by the absolute power of the state (and collectives of states) claim they known better than individuals, families, communities and nations, and the free and spontaneous processes which link them. But the more these absolute powers fail the more they organise. The more they organise the more power they accrue. The more the people fight their power to control the more authoritarian their response.

The destruction of the sovereignty of nations on the altar of a Nazi concept of a "European Community" is merely the latest step in a process which has destroyed the freedom and responsibility of the individual and the associations to which he freely gives allegiance.

There are many groups, some ideological, others pragmatic, which have a vested interest in the destruction of the nation states of Europe - as a prelude to an even more hideous project of "world government". European Fascism, most effectively distilled into the Nazi plans for a European supranational power of the early 1940s, is alive today (at least in its social, economic and "geopolitical" forms) in the institutions of the European Union.

Domestic socialism seeks supranational means of "recapturing" those who have escaped their national controls. International socialism seeks ever more powerful levels of social and economic organisation beyond the control of those national democracies which have so decisively rejected their philosophy. Communism has the pedigree of Lenin's plans for a Europe not dissimilar to the present embryo European "soviet" (Lenin was of course smuggled into Russia in 1917 by the Germans, who also financed him). The former leader of the Soviet Communist Party, Mikhail Gorbachev is now trying to construct a "new world order" in which the kind of globalist power always sought by communism is being made palatable to the corporatists of the West. (Gorbachev's organisation has a base in California).

Corporatists like those listed as attendees at Bilderberg meetings (see Chapters 7 and 8) perhaps have the strongest *economic* interest in the removal of the nation states and the democratic sovereignty of their parliaments. The Trade Unionists, bankers and multinational corporations who have for decades attended the meetings of corporatist "elites" find that linguistic, cultural, parliamentary and religious differences are all barriers to their supranational structures and controls.

There are of course other groups which have an interest in globalist power structures, including many religious and quasi religious organisations. (The Vatican was the first state to recognise the Hitler regime and various modern "churches" have globalist ambitions - including the World Unification

Church or "Moonies", who frequently employ at some expense the speaking skills of Sir Edward Heath).

This book will concentrate on three principal interest groups. First those unions, banks, corporations and industry federations which form the corporatist interest (in particular see chapters 1, 7 and 8). Secondly the Euro-fascist tradition as exemplified by socialists, conservative interventionists and fascists, and in particular continental European politicians with aspirations to create a Catholic European state on a medieval model (chapters 6 and 9). Thirdly the groups and individuals who were either part of the Nazi attempt to create a corporatist European state or supported their activities or just happen to share a similar attitude to corporate and social organisation (chapters 3, 5, 7 and 13).

Chapter 2 will describe how there is scarcely an attribute of at least the social and economic structure of a fascist system which has not been part of the policies of "established" democratic parties as they have embraced and promoted state and corporate power at the expense of the individual, family, community and nation. I hope this particular chapter makes clear the distinction between a people emancipated by democratic freedoms and responsibilities and an elitist system based on business, unions and politicians. This latter system which characterises both the United Kingdom and the European Union today *and* pre-Nazi Germany, is likely to lead to a complete political breakdown and the rise of a dictatorship.

The extent to which the Hitlerian project for Europe has been reproduced by transatlantic corporatism since 1972 was nowhere better demonstrated than in October 1997 when a senior executive of General Motors demanded that the British should abolish the Pound and the Bank of England in favour of the Single European Currency or else the company would close its production in the United Kingdom.

General Motors has a record of political and economic support for European oppression. In 1936 the US ambassador in Berlin complained about that company's "... enormous business here, they complicate things and add to our war dangers." (1) By 1936 General Motors subsidiary Opel was one of the two leading producers of tanks for the Nazi war machine (2) and in 1935 the US War Department protested to the company about its transfer of ethyl lead technology which was so critical in military aircraft. (3)

It is precisely such corporatist power, combined with State control which we fought two world wars to prevent. Now we are threatened by companies who have been guests in Britain for many decades, playing with our 800 year old constitution as they would with a car production line.

As the President of the Norwegian parliament said of the Nazi takeover in 1940: *"What stupefied the Norwegians was how men with whom one had had intimate business relations, who had been cordially welcomed in one's home were in fact agents of destruction."* (4) As this book seeks to demonstrate, the same threats to our nations and democracies now return in the ambitions of multinational corporations.

The American collaboration with the Nazi regime (witting and unwitting) was of a far higher order than that of which the Swiss have been accused - and, unlike Switzerland, the USA was not surrounded by two all-conquering fascist powers.

The parallels between the 1930s and the 1990s in Europe (a kind of political Kondratief cycle) are too clear not to be disturbing, as chapters 10 and 11 describe. The recent introduction of emergency laws in Belgium, in effect suspending the democratic rights of the people, is all too reminiscent of the German Chancellor Heinrich Brüning's similar rule by decree in 1930 - a constitutional device subsequently put to use by Hitler. At least Brüning had to contend with very high unemployment, riots, strikes and popular Nazi and Communist parties. The Eurofanatic Prime Minister of Belgium, Jean Luc Dehaene has no such excuse; his anti-democratic move is designed to squeeze Government borrowing and spending to prepare for the Single European Currency and the abolition of the national currency. But no aim can excuse the means which are (like the entire EU blueprint, structures and methods) blatantly fascist.

Having spent many years living and working in Germany I have known personally many who performed important functions in Nazi occupied Europe. They were very pleasant, personable and idealistic individuals - an impression confirmed by my father who spent several years in prisoner of war camps where he had to co-exist with SS officers. An academic of my own acquaintance excused his Nazi past by saying that "in those days I feared man more than I feared God". Another, a kindly teacher from Belgium, had been in the Gestapo, had been sentenced to death at the end of the war, reprieved and then released in the 1950s before going to teach in Germany.

It was a group of doubtless equally pleasant individuals who formed the "Yugoslav Committee", a circle of Slav intellectuals who wrote the 1915 blueprint for a federal Yugoslavia. Dr Andrew Fear, writing in the European Journal of August 1996, quoted the dangerously naive words of these idealists:

> "Only by uniting all the members of the Yugoslav race and their territories in one independent state can peace be secured for South Eastern Europe."

We now know the tragic results. But as I pointed out in my 1990 pamphlet "Your Country Your Democracy" a similar history lesson could have been learned from the foundation of the nation states of Germany and Italy towards the end of the 19th century. Even where a new federal power was established to rule over principalities speaking the same language and sharing a cultural heritage, there was little organic loyalty to the new German and Italian states. Being unable to rely on such loyalty or even on tax payments to the new national authority, German and Italian governments had to rely on excessive borrowing to fund their federal aspirations. Such instability was undoubtedly a major contributor to inflation, unemployment and the rise of fascism in both countries. A similar federalist venture involving 15 countries with 12 languages and centuries of warfare between them is a fearful prospect. Indeed the only reason the European Union is itself not bankrupt lies in the huge burden of debts its budget demands have imposed on its constituent nations - ironically the chief obstacle to its ambitions for a single currency.

This grave crisis in British and European politics is principally the creation of the German political state which, since its foundation in 1870, has three times waged war against its neighbours. One of the main questions posed in this book is "Have Germany's intentions since 1945 been fundamentally different from those they pursued in the wars since 1870? Or has the same basic strategy been pursued by other means?"

The former chief of the Economic Warfare Section of the US Department of Justice, James Stewart Martin, in his brilliant book *All Honourable Men* was warning, even in 1950, that (5)

> "For whatever reason the larger pattern is a repetition of what followed after World War 1; but the pace has been quicker, as though greater powers were moving more rapidly towards a more catastrophic result."

I devote much space in chapter 3 to discussion of the aims and attitudes of the new democratic Germany of the early 1950s. Like James Martin I was disturbed by what I read of a period so similar to today, before the creation of the East German state, when Germany was bent on re-establishing its political and economic power.

Martin realised in 1950 what this book seeks to bring up to date - that the principal movements which drive the political and economic shape of the world in peace, in the preparations for war, in war and in the treaties which end wars are controlled not so much by democratic governments as by corporatist cliques. When Martin began to dissect the intricate web of international business agreements entered into by the German industrial war machine he found: (6)

> "...arrangements dating back to 1926 and 1929 when international agreements among some of the biggest American, British and German firms had quietly divided up

the world...a business brotherhood more solidly built than *the international finance* of past generations.."

And describing an early version of Bilderberg secrecy, Martin continues (7)

"In mid March 1939 when a group of British and German industrialists gathered at Dusseldorf to map plans for economic collaboration between their two countries, the press barely reported the meetings."

In 1944 Martin and his colleagues investigated how German economic warfare had been conducted: (8)

"In three years we had prepared thirty six hundred of these snapshots of German economic power in action...a picture of an enemy that could survive a military defeat because it did not need or use military weapons."

In other words the enemy machine was a corporate machine with covert international allies and if: (9)

"The period between the wars was only an armistice during which the firms of Germany conducted war against us.."

then was not the same thing happening after the second world war aided, or even driven, by American corporations and American Government policy? Certainly there was ample evidence for such a claim. American Attorney General Francis Biddle warned: (10)

"The companies which were used as instruments to violate the peace treaties, to dominate industry in Europe, to support the Nazi war machine and to restrict production here will then appear in the guise of ordinary commercial firms."

Biddle went on to warn about those very policies pursued by US governments since 1945 and which have reached their disastrous climax in the Bush and Clinton administrations' appeasement of German domination in Europe and the support of international corporatism in its vendetta against sovereign nation states. The anti-democratic role of state and corporate power, so well demonstrated in the activities of supranational elites like the Bilderberg Group, fall neatly into the pattern of corporate dominance of German democracy. Francis Biddle succinctly describes this long established process: (11)

> "The pattern of the activities of these firms was established before the Nazis came to power and during the early days of the German Republic. The German Government and the German people as a whole have never accepted the doctrines of economic liberalism which run through American history. The monopolistic firms of Germany have survived in that country through two wars and constitute a definite menace to the future peace of the world. As long as they survive in their present form it will be exceedingly difficult to develop independent industry in Europe outside of Germany."

But the intended post war clearance of these corporate cartels was abandoned and the establishment of a European Union in which monopolistic *national* corporations could be defended by reference to the larger "European market" have further frustrated these laudible aims. Indeed the European Union has permitted those very countries which were part of the Nazi corporatist European economy to override many market initiatives of the European Commission - steel, coal, computers, shipbuilding and airlines being classic examples of state manipulation.

Although Biddle's warnings were heeded to some extent when the industrial arm of the German war machine, I G Farben and a number of other combines were broken up, the whole process was brought to a halt by a *volte face* by the American administration, represented on the ground by General Clay. The heavy industrial combines were ignored and an emphasis put on purely consumer markets. Then as now the principal enemies of a free trading society were not so much the overt foreign enemy but covert domestic "friends".

When Martin arrived in Germany he found that the Director of the Economics Division of the future Government of occupied Germany was a Colonel Graeme K. Howard. (12)

> "Howard was the author of a book, written in 1940....called *America and the New World Order* (note the same code words used today - RA), an apologia for the Nazi economic system that might just as well have been titled *You can do Business with Hitler*."

Although this particular individual was subsequently dismissed many of those who worked in the Allied governance of Germany came from those prominent banks which had financed the Nazi government and corporate machine throughout the 1930s and even up to 1941.

It is important to note two points about the German attitude to "Europe" between the wars and the true economic relationship between the defeated Germany and the economic situation of its enemies. Martin shows that Alsace Lorraine in France was the historical centre of the West European steel industry, not the Ruhr. France possessed the iron ore and the steel plant. After its conquest of France in 1870 Germany occupied Alsace Lorraine and began to "integrate" (another euphemism in currency today) those French assets into the German Ruhr economy. The blast furnaces were near the ore supplies in Lorraine and most of the coke works were near the coal supplies in the Ruhr. The Treaty of Versailles required that Germany deliver to France 7m tons of coal per annum - about half of the 1913 level - but even this they failed to do until the Allies agreed to pay $1 in gold per ton of coal shipped. The argument used then to hoodwink naive Europeans and gullible Americans was that Germany needed help to preserve *European* industry. Then as now, when German industry and government had an interest the project became of "European" not German interest. When Germany lost the steel conquests of 1870 they became the "European" issue of the 1920s. When German military and corporate conquest of other countries failed in the 1940s, the same aims became a matter of "European integration" in the post war period.

Although the terms of the Treaty of Versailles were onerous, there were many ways in which Germany - and in particular

German industry - benefited from post war conditions. One way in which the German corporate tail wagged the government dog was in the hundreds of millions of Reichsmarks paid to iron and steel companies by the German state to compensate for returning the Lorraine steel plants to their rightful owners. This huge subsidy was a major contributor to the economic instability of Germany's own making. Furthermore there had been no major industrial damage to German industry in the First War - surrender took place when German forces were still fighting outside their own borders. France on the other hand suffered considerable industrial losses - Verdun being a major steel centre as well as a battleground. German industry therefore got a head start over France with German government subsidies for coal and steel and for iron ore imports from Sweden, Spain and Canada - anywhere other than France! This was of course a further blow to French industry. German railways raised massive charges for transporting what little coal was delivered to France and the post war coal shortage boosted the German economy at the expense of the French.

While extracting the $1 of gold per ton of coal exports to France in order to "feed their starving workers", German industry was busy constructing an entire new complex of iron and steel plants and the state was re-arming apace. In addition the Treaty of Versailles required large loans to Germany from Allied banks.

The 1923 French occupation of the Ruhr in order to exact the Treaty obligation of coal deliveries was therefore not a surprise. Nor perhaps was the supply of millions of tons of British coal to Germany and criticism of the French government by the British!

Furthermore, far from being the weak industrial power of Europe, Germany took advantage of the post war coal scarcity to organise a steel cartel which prevented genuine competition from Belgium and France and took the lead in establishing and then dominating the International Steel Cartel even though (like so many of the European Union's institutions) it was based in Luxembourg.

The post Second World War Allied government of Germany found this pattern repeating itself but, despite the efforts of analysts like James Stewart Martin, corporate and political pressure from Britain and America (combined with a military administration ignorant of industrial markets) allowed many corporatist structures to survive the "denazification" programme as successfully as did many Nazis. Many executives in the Economic Warfare Section of the Department of Justice resigned when General Clay overturned the entire anti-corporatist strategy in the name of "European" industrial recovery (Speer and other Nazis had their effect on American thinking - see below). *This was done even in contravention of the laws which the Allied regime had itself enacted.* Martin notes that: (13)

> "In the end this left a handful of Americans responsible for the trade practices of twenty million Germans in the United States Zone....Not only was the main job left undone, but public servants were damned for having tried to do it."

But the mistakes of this era were not just sins of omission but of commission. In May 1948 General Clay approved a plan to allow privately controlled industry associations (active and dominant to this day at least in wage bargaining) each with its headquarters at the centre of their respective industries. Membership would be "voluntary" but all companies would come under the aegis of these organisations. They would control and co-ordinate the industries concerned requiring the submission of production and sales data and allocation of scarce materials. This was in fact in direct contradiction of an earlier Allied policy and all too exact a reproduction of the "Reichsgruppe Industrie" which had enjoyed such excellent relations with the British "Federation of British Industry" before the war.

Indeed the British were no less helpful to German industry after the war. The British Control Commission's director of economic affairs, Sir Percy Mills, said of various unsavoury businessmen who had run the Nazi industrial machine: (14)

> "What's wrong with them? They were not Nazis they are businessmen."

It is a mistake to apply to those who are an integral part of state and corporate power the same logic we apply to responsible individuals. An individual is responsible for his actions, a corporatist is part of a machine he does not control, set on a course which even the directors did not necessarily decide. An individual can only extract money (legally) from himself, the corporatist can exploit his distant shareholders and the monopolist his customers, just as the politician can exploit the taxpayer. An individual would enquire about the motivations of those who organise meetings and wonder why they should be held in secret. The corporatist will not enquire about motivations of a corporation and will accept secrecy among those who seem to have important corporate titles and positions in a government. An individual has the responsibility for moral judgment, the corporatist can excuse his collaboration with immoral men as "for the corporate good" or as "just doing business and earning a profit", or in the last resort he can blame the "majority".

James Martin, writing of his experiences of corporatist intrigue affecting the government of the American Zone of Germany, concluded that: (15)

> "We had not been stopped in Germany by German business but by American business. The forces which had stopped us had operated from the United States but had not operated in the open."

Just as the German people had been governed in the 1930s not by parliament but by presidential decree which bypassed parliament and today the British people are governed by Brussels directives which bypass Westminster, so Martin realised in 1950 that: (16)

"We were not stopped by laws of Congress....whatever it was that had stopped us was not "the Government". But it clearly had command of channels through which the Government normally operates."

Just as this book identifies Bilderberg and other corporatist "elites" as the principal enemies of democracy and national sovereignty since the 1950s, so Martin from his senior and pivotal position within the immediate post war governance of Germany concluded that between the wars "national governments stood on the sidelines while bigger operators arranged the world's affairs".

It is the decades-long continuation of this secretive and anti-democratic process which has brought Britain and Europe to their present crisis. A war has been waged by individuals and corporations within the United Kingdom and without, within Europe and in the USA - a war without guns or planes or ships. The covert forces of corporatist and State power are poised for victory in the subjugation of individuals, families and nations whose only justification as democratic agents is the freedom and responsibility which the corporatists would deny them. There is no longer time for argument. The lines are drawn and battle must be joined; but the victory of free men and nations is by no means assured.

(1) Edgar B. Nixon, ed., *Franklin D. Roosevelt and Foreign Affairs*, Vol III, Cambridge, Mass., 1969.

(2) Professor Anthony Sutton, *Wall Street and the Rise of Hitler*, Bloomfield Books, 1976, page 31.

(3) United States Congress, Senate Hearings before the Subcommittee on Military Affairs, Scientific and technical mobilisation 78th Congress First Session, S.702, GPO 1944.

(4) Winston Churchill, *The History of the Second World War*, Vol 1, page 546.

(5) Martin, James Stewart, *All Honourable Men*, McClelland & Stewart Canada and USA 1950, preface.

(6) op cit page 5

(7) ibid
(8) op cit page 14
(9) ibid
(10) op cit page 15
(11) op cit page 15-16
(12) op cit page 24
(13) op cit page 262
(14) op cit page 90
(15) op cit page 264
(16) ibid

1

SOCIALISM, CORPORATISM AND THE ESSENCE OF FASCISM

This book makes three claims. Firstly that the coercive power of the state and collectives supported by the state are as attractive to corporatist (ie non individual) capitalists as they are to socialists and that the combination of these two movements in a corporatist state is in fact the essence of social and economic fascism.

Secondly this stage of social and economic fascism (because of the enormous strains it puts on the organic structures of a free society like the free and responsible individual, family, community and nation) brings about political and military fascism, which then threaten both domestic peace and the freedoms of other nations.

Thirdly that all modern "democratic" capitalist societies have become so corporatist that, through international corporatist institutions like the European Union, free peoples and nations are threatened *even before* political and military fascism have developed and that this leads to the same international threats to freedom and democracy as overt military power would have produced.

This chapter deals with the first two claims by analysing how corporatist capitalism and socialism were the two indispensable ingredients in the prelude to and in the reality of German fascism of the 1930s and 1940s.

It is customary for both socialist and capitalist political parties to deny that fascism had anything to do with their own philosophies. Socialists are the most vehement in their denials since they have traditionally used the term as an insult for their opponents. During the Nuremberg trials American corporatist capitalists were anxious to distance themselves from their undeniable industrial support in the 1930s of those German corporations (like the Dresdner Bank, the electricity giant AEG or IG Farben) most associated with the Nazi regime.

While socialists tried to deny the blatant socialist appeal of the Nazis to the German working class, corporatist capitalists ignored the undeniable strong financial and managerial connections between German industry and the Nazi state and government favouritism shown to large financial institutions and armament manufacturers often at the cost of entrepreneurs, small businesses and farmers.

But the seeds of fascism were sown in the 1920s when "centre" parties of the Christian right, the Liberal Party and the (initially radical) Social Democratic Party repeatedly abandoned their individual voters in the pursuit of the collectivist interests of the state, the party, the unions or big business. "Moderate" parties established the kind of corporatist institutions which both inevitably led to Adolf Hitler *and* provided him with the political and economic structures and often the legal precedents to run his dictatorship.

It was during the First World War that many of the causes of future resentment among the Germans arose. Many small businesses, suffering from lack of labour and unable to benefit from large government contracts or even to obtain raw materials, were bankrupted. Much of the middle class was "proletarianised" while other German businesses found, after the war, that Jews fleeing persecution further East (the "Ostjuden" as the Nazis called them) had established businesses and taken over traditional German markets. The result, as one analyst of the period observed was that: (1)

> "A middle class revolutionary spirit equally hostile to the Stock Exchange and Marxism began to flourish."

The post war revolutionary movement swept away the monarchy, denigrated the nation and seemed to put the working class in control of the middle classes who had lost so much during the war. State war contracts and the urgent need after the war to earn foreign exchange to pay reparations benefited the large corporations and capital concentration in the state-approved cartels further alienated the middle classes. The socialist state was followed by the corporatist state.

As if this were not bad enough there followed the great inflation of the 1920s which further benefited the twin pillars of a corporatist society - the state (as the biggest debtor of all) and the large corporations whose quotation on the (inflation boosted) stock exchange and their borrowing power allowed them to actually profit from high inflation. In addition major corporations and the banks held large amounts of foreign exchange which appreciated considerably as the *Reichsmark* fell dramatically.

In the face of this manifest injustice the Government, far from acting to protect impoverished individuals legislated to protect those who exploited them. As Taylor points out: (2)

> "A couple who owned a large house before the war and received an income from letting the rooms would find that in 1923 the cost of replacing a broken pane of glass was more than all the rent they had ever received from their tenants since the level of rents was fixed while plate glass prices were not."

There could not be a clearer case of state-supported corporate power over the individual. One price which did not rise in anywhere near the proportions of inflation between 1921 and 1923 was the price charged by the banks for their money (the banks had other ways of profiting). Vast profits were therefore to be made by borrowing Reichsmarks one week and repaying at a much depreciated rate the next. The banks were of course the biggest borrowers and they lent to the large companies who had overseas earnings and (ever appreciating) physical assets as security. In addition the banks took shares in the companies to which they were lending - a practice still prevalent in German banking today but which in the inflationary 1920s was another source of considerable profit.

As the banks benefited from the effect of inflation, the savings of the middle class were decimated. The increasing concentration of business activity (the State actually enforcing cartel agreements by law) to the detriment of the smaller traders and manufacturers caused more resentment and further enhanced the power of the corporatist state. The official cartels in steel, coal, cement, plate glass and chemicals were then increasingly matched by small producer cooperatives and even buyer cooperatives. In Germany by 1925 combines controlled 93% of mining, 95% of steel and 87% of electricity. 70% of the capital of *all* German companies was in the hands of a mere 2,000 firms. Once the collectivist process is established then those excluded by such political power in commercial markets have no choice - they must either succumb or adopt similar corporatist structures themselves.

We see the same process in the world at large since the European Union started its collectivist controls of agriculture and latterly of industrial trade. The rest of the world finds it necessary to establish competing collectivist systems and therefore forms the economic blocks which then lead to dangerous international friction. Trading blocks, whether within countries in the form of corporatist cartels and state monopolies or internationally in the form of trading blocks always start with the claim that they are *freeing* economic activity. But even if they reduce protectionism between the limited number of companies or countries *within* their agreement (EU, NAFTA) they are in fact establishing worse relations with those *outside*.

This logic is best demonstrated in the term *Single* European Market, which for those who believe in open and free trade is, of course, a contradiction in terms. The Single European

Market is however the construction not of nationists and free traders but of corporatist politicians bent on creating a *single* state with a *single* government, a *single* civil service, etc. etc. Indeed it is the practice of corporatism *within* countries which leads corporate capital - and the socialist trade unions who bargain with them, and the corporatist state which subsidises them - to extend the principle to the *supranational* level. The ultimate step is the extinction of the nations and their parliaments and the transfer of power to a level so geographically, culturally and democratically remote that individual voters cannot influence events. Corporations can go straight to the source of power - the state's bureaucrats and politicians.

As profitable for the German corporations which had benefited from the great inflation in the 1920s was the subsequent currency reform and revaluation. But now even those bourgeois interests like the small farmer who had benefited from being able to raise debt against the security of his land were decimated by the reverse process - their debts, in the absence of inflation, became a real burden (just as they are today for British houseowners left with excessively high mortgages taken out in times of high inflation). In theory of course small savers should have benefited from the currency reform as their loans to others should have been repaid in "real" money. It is yet another proof of the power of corporatism in 1920s Germany that this elementary justice was opposed by large corporations and the government restricted the revaluation to only 15% of the original gold mark value. Indeed the government postponed indefinitely the revalorisation of its own debts to the public!

After this corporatist attack on the individual the middle classes revolted in the elections of 1924 with the so-called "Fighting League of Beggars" (!) doing particularly well. It was the "centre" and "liberal" parties which had deserted their own voters by supporting the corporatist state (much like the two major parties in Britain today) which suffered most. However the German Nationalist Party, which had done well in the elections, then supported a coalition headed by the very man responsible for the revaluation scandal - Hans Luther.

The conflict for the German middle classes and the independent, non collectivist, members of all classes in the 1920s was the same as their equivalents in Britain today - they had Hobson's choice between several corporatist parties which represented the "mainstream" and two major fringe parties - the Communists and the Nazi Party which gained membership rapidly as soon as the crisis deepened and the so-called "moderate" parties showed every sign of supporting the status quo. Pearl S. Buck summed up the choice neatly: (3)

> "The Holzmans came to visit us. What Germany needs said father to Mr Holzman is a sound and healthy middle class and what the middle class needs is a strong middle class party. Mr Holzman, a member of the Social Democratic party said 'It would be wiser for you to side with the workers against the monopolies.' Father replied 'Good if only the workers would side with us instead of striking against us.'
>
> The von Bulows also came to visit us and father repeated 'What Germany needs is a sound and healthy middle class and what the middle class needs is a strong middle class party' To this Mr von Bulow, a member of the German National party, replied 'We have already more than enough parties as it is. Why don't you side with us. We shall see that law and order are restored at the port'. Father said 'But who guarantees to us that you won't swallow us after we have checked the workers?' "

How easily could that father have the same conversation today with a member of the Labour Party representing the corporatism of state and union power, of high taxes and inflation, and a member of the Conservative Party representing the corporatism of state and private monoplies, high taxes, high inflation, subsidised city institutions, and the Confederation of British Industry with its contempt for the nation which once defined the very essence of Conservatism. Or perhaps the father could have confronted a member of the Liberal Party with its own middle class collectivism, disdain for the nation state, and a prime mover in the destruction, by the new "Europe", of the sovereignty of parliament.

The extent to which traditionally stable and loyal middle class voters can turn against those associated with the power of the state can be seen in 1920s Germany. When both the Socialists and the Communists proposed to expropriate the estates of the German princes the nationalists and the bourgeois parties opposed them. But the various associations of "savers and debtors" with their justified grievances against a government which sided with big business interests refused to oppose the socialists' proposal. (4)

> "They argued that there was no fundamental difference between legal expropriation (of the princes) and de facto expropriation through inflation (of themselves)."

In the United Kingdom today a similar process has been under way. As inflation (with which organised labour could keep pace, but which impoverished the small trader and businessman), gave way to a recession and low inflation which burdened the mortgaged house-owner, these (traditionally loyal) classes turned against the British monarchy. Indeed had the British middle classes not benefited from the irresponsible government subsidy of the house price boom, a similar rejection of the traditional parties might have already occurred in the United Kingdom as it did in 1920s Germany.

What was termed in Germany "the silent socialisation of the small trader" has its equivalent today as the independent small business owner becomes dependent on the handouts from the very state which has impoverished his business. Many small and even large businesses find it profitable to rent property not to their fellow citizens but to the state. A recent House of Commons report pointed to the scandalous profits made by landlords in London where housing benefit for the poor (many being illegal immigrants) was paid by the state direct to landlords.

Another corporatist parallel with pre-Hitler Germany is the state subsidy of large landowners and companies at the expense of the individual. Tax allowances for pension funds which invest in quoted companies, export credit guarantees, inflation and agricultural "set aside" payments all unduly discriminate in favour of the large enterprise.

1920s Germany witnessed massive profits made by large industrial and financial corporations out of the great inflation, the currency reform scandal, the concentration of capital, state approved legal cartels and the "Osthilfe scandal" in which state subsidies for businesses had been channelled into private coffers.

In recent years in the United Kingdom a similar corporatist corruption has been evident. Government ministers have retired from parliament to take up directorships and chairmanships in companies whose directors had become very wealthy by the (monopolised) form of privatisation chosen by those very ministers when in office. Massive government subsidies for pension funds (and lax legislation) led to corruption by businessmen who saw a honey pot of tax free funds. The most infamous of these cases was when some £600m of pensioners' money was fraudulently converted by Robert Maxwell, the former Labour MP. A similar but perhaps even more widespread corruption arose out of the large government subsidies for house mortgages. Many solicitors up and down the country have been found guilty of mortgage fraud.

A more direct equivalent to the German "Osthilfe" scandal is the continuous corruption in the Common Agricultural Policy which costs the European Community - and hence the British taxpayer as the second biggest financier of its budget - some £4 billion per annum. Whether at national or supranational level state subsidies and control mean corruption on a massive scale. It is as true in the United Kingdom today as it was in Germany of the 1920s.

But of equal significance in both periods is the role of corporations which influence - and are subsidised by - the state. In the United Kingdom a Conservative Party which has lost the support of its individual members (membership has fallen by more than 50% since 1990 and by 80% since the 1950s) has turned to its corporate donors for funds. As a result it is corporations which have been the most influential agents in forming Conservative Party policy. This has been most graphically illustrated in legislation on Sunday trading, gambling laws and on relations with the European Union. Policies which would not have had the support of the Conservative Party were passed by a Conservative government relying on the help of Labour and Liberal Democrat votes.

This chapter set out to demonstrate that fascism in its economic and social structures unites both state socialism and corporatist capitalism. Fascism is not just another alternative to the various political movements within a democratic system; it is an alternative to the entire democratic system itself. By taking the worst of both socialism and capitalism it constructs a powerful collectivist state in which the individual has no role except as a devotee of an approved movement or corporate body. This combination naturally produced tensions within that party which benefited from the crisis of 1920s German corporatism and which took over its structures - the NSDAP (National Socialist German Workers Party) or Nazi Party.

These tensions were evident in their public pronouncements. In response to a transport strike the Nazis in Saxony played the corporatist card: (5)

> "absolute opposition to any form of industrial sabotage."

while the party in Berlin played the socialist card:

> "unconditional solidarity with the workers"

Some party organs criticised those who wish to abolish capitalism:

> "abolition of the capitalist system has for centuries been nothing more than a catchphrase ... nothing is more unjust than equality"

while others attacked *international* corporatism:

> "The Frankfurter Allgemeine, central organ of the international finance hyenas."

Here is the point about Hitler's fascism. He did not object to corporatism, only to international corporatism and the "imperialist" Anglo Saxon trading system. He did not object to *national* socialism, only to international socialism and Marxism.

Before we go on to analyse the socialist elements in fascism there is one further element in late 1920s Germany which finds its echo in the United Kingdom today - taxation and the alienation of traditional Conservative voters. We have already observed how the end of an inflationary period puts an enormous burden on borrowers. The biggest borrower, the state, benefits to the tune of billions of pounds as inflation reduces the burden of its debt, but in non inflationary times it must resort to taxation to recoup what inflation would otherwise have financed. A Nazi leaflet of 1930 took advantage of the resulting resentment of the tax payer: (6)

> "The tax screw is being turned ever tighter. You are the helots of this system. Your only job is to work and pay taxes which go into the salaries and pensions of ministers."

Even after the 26% pay rise which MPs awarded themselves today's Conservative government would call this the "lack of a feelgood factor", although they have not understood why this should be so. The explanation is simple enough. The government not long ago raised taxation by a record 7p in the pound and the fruits of all the economic growth are going towards paying off the debts of the government and the debts of the over-borrowed house owner. *Apparently* low inflation is no more than (non monopolistic) traders, squeezed by depressed consumer spending, being unable to pass on higher costs in the form of higher prices.

The extent to which the Conservative Party in Britain is now very much a corporatist party can be seen in the kind of issue on which Conservative MPs take a stand. One MP, an unequivocal supporter of European Union legislation which has destroyed the democratic and parliamentary rights of the British electorate, recently resigned not for any constitutional reason or to defend the individual rights of his constituents, but because he had lost a vote in parliament which tried to allow local newspaper groups (in which industry he was previously employed) to bid for television franchises.

In similar vein, after 10 years of supreme indifference to the health of British beef consumers, John Major suddenly took up arms against the European Community for banning British beef exports. The loss to businesses and to the Exchequer due to lost beef markets was far more important for this corporatist Prime Minister than either British consumers or the European Union's power over the British constitution.

It is precisely such corporatist policies which have destroyed the Conservative middle classes and enhanced the wealth of collectivist socialists (whose state and unionised power need not be troubled by market forces). As a result the British Labour Party in the 1990s is now wealthy enough to elect a quasi Conservative leader. In 1920s Germany the socialist *in work*, being relatively well off, stayed with the Social Democratic Party which often took a conservative line - compared to the Nazi party or the Communist party (KPD), (85% of whose members in 1932 were unemployed), both of which advocated far more radical solutions.

Indeed the confrontations between the Nazi and Communist parties on the streets in Germany disguised a closer political connection than one might suppose. They often supported strikes which other parties opposed, they supported certain expropriation policies and when 54% of the KPD's membership left in 1932, a very large number went to join the Nazi party.

It is therefore not surprising - despite the denials of many socialist revisionists - that the Nazi party fully warranted its name as the party with "socialist" and "workers" in its name. Hitler himself had joined the German Workers Party in 1919 and added the words "German" and "National" in an attempt to win over many working class nationalists.

A 1920 Nazi leaflet declared its working class socialist philosophy: (7)

> "I am a workmate ... a socialist like yourselves and want manual workers to gain equality with all creative groups and I want the confiscation of profits earned without work or effort. I still hope for a true and just form of socialism, the salvation of the working masses and the freeing of creative mankind from the chains of exploitative capitalism."

In 1921 the NSDAP merged with the German Socialist Party and the socialist direction of the party was in no doubt in an election leaflet published in 1925:

> "For years you sweated so that the State can pay interest on its loan capital. You are damned for all eternity to be wage slaves if you do not demand the nationalisation of the banks and the money economy, the abolition of interest exploiters and stock exchange speculators and the abolition of mobile share capital."

Goebbels (from the North German, more socialist part of the NSDAP) at first cursed Hitler as a "reactionary" but after meeting him proclaimed him "a great man". The socialist stance was reflected in other leaflets: (8)

> "our people have been sold out into the hands of international world capital. Do you want this to go on for ever? - then vote for the capitalist parties."

A similar approach by the Labour Party in Britain has always been characterised by reference to the evils of "multinationals" and the iniquity of privatising state industries only for them to be bought by foreign corporations. Indeed in a recent xenophobic attack on the leader of the British Referendum Party (Sir James Goldsmith, whose mother was French and who is Jewish) the Labour MP Tony Banks screamed hysterically from the backbenches about a "foreign millionaire" while similar language emanates from the corporatist Conservative Party. When last in office the Labour Party had draconian controls on the export of capital and their attacks on capital ownership were evident in high taxation on interest and dividend income and inheritance as well as controls on dividends paid.

But just as the modern Labour Party has revised its socialism so did Hitler. In 1927 he clarified Article 17 of the Party programme on nationalisation, just as the Labour Party has now revised its Clause 4. Hitler explained that the "expropriation of land for communal purposes without compensation" did not mean that the NSDAP did not accept the principle of private property but only property illegally acquired or companies not run to the benefit of the community. How reminiscent of Mr Blair's approach to privatised monopolies. Far from renationalising, or even introducing competition, the Labour Party will levy a windfall profits tax on the monopolies - thus joining in the exploitation of consumers.

1990s Labour and 1920s Nazism recognised the power of capitalist markets and, far from destroying them, they would take advantage of them in order to enhance the power of the central state. This they (rightly) saw as a more efficient way of manipulating economic affairs for political ends.

There is another crucial comparison between 1990s British "socialism" and 1920s German fascism - the power of a managerial elite with loyalty only to the leadership. Taylor describes the Nazi party: (9)

> "... a leadership core emerged whose bureaucratic ability and absolute loyalty to Hitler meant they were content with a managerial role within a rigid hierarchy and less prone to

challenge the leadership over fundamental issues of party policy."

The following NSDAP leaflet could easily have been produced by the modern Labour Party. (10)

> "Man should not be valued according to his money rather according to his accomplishments for the community. The common good before individual greed, that is socialism... out with the swindle Marxism and away with bourgeois selfishness."

The final link in the Nazi chain of interest groups was the alienated small businesses, retailers and peasant farmers. Much as in early 1990s Britain, the turnover of small shops fell between 1928 and 1932 by one third with 40,000 small businesses collapsing in 1930 alone. As in Britain under John Major (where unemployment benefit has been cut from 12 months to 6 months, thus leaving those with any savings, and therefore no social security, with no means of support - until they have nothing!) so in the early 1930s German unemployment benefit was cut from 6 months to 6 weeks.

But the Nazis' solutions to these results of corporatism were not libertarian and democratic or anti state. On the contrary their solution was more state involvement, more controls of markets and competition. For instance they formed the Militant Association of Retailers. Taylor summarises their aims: (11)

> "The association promised there would be a return to a form of medieval guild economy in which competition would be controlled by corporate bodies in place of an economic system determined by market forces."

Like the causes of the chaos which preceded the appointment of Hitler, the solutions are only too typical of "moderate" political parties in Britain and Europe today. Each interest group's solution involves the power of the state on the side of that group, using collective power in precisely the same way as those who brought the crisis about.

Today this corporatist conspiracy of the so called "centre parties" has alienated the same groups as in 1920s Germany and the increasing support for neo-fascist parties in Italy, Germany and France is accompanied by the thuggery of the extreme left. The marches of the former, running the gauntlet of the latter are as regular a feature of the 1990s as they were of the 1920s. Indeed in Germany the attacks on foreigners, the rise of Nazism in the armed forces, the burning of immigrants' homes and the utter contempt for what the press laughably calls the "moderate" parties is a prelude to the resurgence of dictatorial politics and social violence on a grand scale - made undoubtedly easier by the "freedom of movement of European citizens"!

In France where, like Germany, unemployment is over 12% (double that among the under 25s) the unemployed have rioted, burned 600 cars in Strassbourg (that legal centre of the new Eurostate) and attacked unemployment offices. Urban violence has quadrupled in 4 years and the National Front has obtained over 15% of the national vote and up to 26% regionally.

The collapse into extremism can only be prevented by an alternative, regional, democratic anti corporatist leadership in Germany, France and Europe in general (and based on sackable and comprehensible national democracies), but as economic and social events gather pace the demagoguery of a new *Fuehrer* is a far quicker and more easily understood route for desperate people.

The violence of the state even in apparently "democratic" regimes, never mind in a Hitlerian dictatorship, can maintain their hegemony for a long time - especially with the distractions of overseas conquest and sundry invasions. (The British "beef war" is a not unrelated phenomenon.)

As a further example of how "liberal" political parties can put in place the dangerous constitutional structures which will subsequently be used by their enemies we can compare the Conservative government's signing of various European Community Treaties under "Crown Prerogative" with

Germany's President Heinrich Brüning (of the Christian Centre Party) who in 1930 was able to rule by presidential decree. Both processes allowed "democratic" governments to bypass the parliamentary process. In Germany the device was most useful to Hitler to effectively destroy the spirit of the constitution, just as the Major government at Maastricht effectively destroyed the spirit and letter of the British constitution.

Yet another aspect of supreme weakness which helped the rise of Hitler in Germany was the system of proportional representation which caused a splintering of democratic parties. Needless to say the same system, supported by the Labour and Liberal parties, may soon be introduced into Britain, just as the more chaotic political systems of the world are appreciating the stability which the British majority system of voting has conferred. It was the collapse in 1930 of the "Grand Coalition" which PR systems often make necessary which hastened the takeover by the Nazi Party. Indeed in 1969 after another Grand Coalition came to an end it was the Nazi successor party the NPD which came within 0.7% of taking 30 seats in the German Bundestag.

After his appointment by Hindenburg to the Chancellorship Hitler deliberately failed to form a coalition and forced new elections. As Goebbels remarked of fighting an election as a government party: (12)

> "Radio and Press are at our disposal, even money is not lacking."

Indeed it was not, for, just before the election, leading industrialists were invited to Goering's palace and kindly donated three million Reichsmarks to the NSDAP. Just as the present British CBI can be guaranteed to be first in line when a threat to the democratic rights and economic interests of the British electorate is in prospect, so their German equivalents in 1933 were the first to support the corporatist state. Indeed in the declaration of Thyssen, Krupp, Siemens, Bosch and Schacht to Hindenburg, the German equivalents of the CBI managed to appeal to both nationalists and socialists: (13)

> "We recognise in the national movement which has penetrated our people the beginning of an era which through the overcoming of class contrasts creates the essential basis for a rebirth of the German economy."

Shortly after the election victory the so-called "Enabling Bill" was passed by a two thirds majority and by the end of the year 150,000 political prisoners were in concentration camps.

I have tried to demonstrate in this chapter that fascism is not an exotic quirk of politics, associated only with fanatical dictators. Rather it is a set of ideas which the major "democratic" parties share in varying degrees and indeed whose social and economic structures they themselves, often unwittingly, put in place. The enormous strains which they thereby put on free economic and political systems as well as on the individual then lead to the collapse of the parliamentary state. Their successors, adopting the structures already in place, then take the process on to the political and military stages of fascism, or, as in the modern European Union, supranational collectivist structures become so powerful that the conquests of war are achieved through the "peaceful" signing of treaties and the imposition of directives and regulation.

It is no coincidence that the parallels between 1920s and 1930s Germany and 1980s and 1990s Britain are so strong. As this book will demonstrate, the same ideas, the same philosophy, the same socio economic principles, often the same individuals and corporations and the same kind of politicians have dominated both periods.

(1) Simon Taylor, *Germany 1918-1933*, Duckworth 1983 Page 47
(2) Taylor, op cit page 53
(3) Pearl S. Buck *How it happens: talk among the German People 1914-1944*, New York 1947.
(4) Taylor, op cit page 58
(5) Taylor, op cit page 94 and 96
(6) Taylor, op cit page 85

(7) Taylor, op cit page 63
(8) Taylor, op cit page 78
(9) Taylor, op cit page 86
(10) Taylor, op cit page 90
(11) Taylor, op cit page 98
(12) Nuremberg Trials Document PS 3901
(13) Taylor, op cit page 121

2

FASCIST ELEMENTS IN BRITISH POLITICAL PARTIES

> An interview at Conservative Central Office:
> **Journalist:** "I am not a natural Tory voter, in fact I am more drawn to Labour ..." **Tory candidate interviewer:** "Don't worry about that, there are lots of us who have the sort of views that could pass for either. We can make perfectly good careers." (1)

When Norman Tebbit and Tony Blair make common cause with a privatised monopoly (British Telecom) in its attempt to obtain special privileges from the State and when Robin Cook recommends using British ambassadors to represent British business, then we may feel like George Orwell's animals at the end of "Animal Farm" who, looking through the farmhouse window, are unable to distinguish between the revolutionary pigs and the old farmer with whom the pigs have now made a pact.

But such scenes should be no surprise, for the corporatist conservative has always had much in common with the state socialist and the system which unites them is socio-economic fascism.

It is a dangerous conceit to imagine that the ideological diseases which affect our enemies have not, to some degree at least, permeated our own society. It is equally dangerous to assume that a "fascist" is someone who persecutes political opponents, exterminates Jews and gypsies, conquers foreign countries and greets his friends with an extravagant salute.

Many of the political beliefs and economic and social structures of Germany and Italy in the 1930s and of Spain up to the mid-1970s were either based on, or have subsequently been mimicked by, "democratic" governments - indeed by the very governments who waged war against fascism. Hitler saw his "Drang nach Osten" as the equivalent of America's "Westward Ho!", his state socialist interventions as the equivalent of Roosevelt's "New Deal" and the Volkswagen as his Model T Ford.

Hitler's persecution of the Jews and Slavs had its historical equivalence in the American annihilation of the Red Indians. When that great "liberal", Thomas Jefferson, regretted an Indian fight-back against the white man's "law" he wrote: "I had hoped the Red Indian would have been integrated into the new nation. It looks like they must be exterminated". During the 1930s 15 American states had eugenics laws not dissimilar to Nazi Germany's.

Both Hitler and Mussolini regarded communistic forms of state ownership as foolish and inefficient and realised that the state could manipulate the people, control industry and enhance its power without wholesale nationalisation. High government spending and taxes, manipulation of savings and investment, monetary control and state-directed spending on welfare and the goods and services of private companies - all proved to be far more efficient tools of control.

Today we see all these elements in the "democratic" governance of the USA and Western Europe. So-called "Conservative" parties have for decades become ever more statist and dirigiste while socialists have become ever more conscious of the power of capitalist markets. The right has recognised and been tempted by the power and patronage of the state (even using privatisation as a means of maximising state revenue) and the left has seen the massive effects of state interventions on sensitive market mechanisms. **As the right has moved to the left and the left to the right they have met in the very forms of social and economic manipulation favoured by fascism.**

For the Conservative, state spending is acceptable if it comes in the form of tax "incentives", the state purchase of defence and infrastructure and purchases financed by the nationalised lottery. For the Socialist, capitalist markets provide the wealth with which they can buy social obedience and the freedom for trade unions to "bargain" for the wealth of capitalism - while still enjoying state protection for their monopoly power.

For both ideologies, basking in the power of corporatism, it is useful to allow market forces (from which they largely exempt themselves and their friends) to eliminate, or severely restrict, the small business, entrepreneur, shopkeeper or farmer. Such individualism might seek to challenge state power if (manipulated) market forces did not keep them poor - or permanently dependent on the state for their incomes. Stalin might have used this more subtle power against the free peasants of Russia - the effect would have been almost as devastating as the massacres.

Although it is the violent language and political legacy of Hitler and Mussolini which we recall today it is more likely that such antics were the characteristics not of strong but of weak personalities. So weak that they could only assert a "manly" image of themselves through social hatred, state power and collectivist coercion.

In Friedrich Reck-Malleczewen's brilliant diary of the Nazi period (he was shot at Dachau in 1945) he describes being in a Munich restaurant when Hitler entered alone and took a neighbouring table. (2)

> "His face took on the sullen expression of a minor bureaucrat who has ventured into a place which he would not generally enter but now that he is there demands for his good money that he be served and treated every bit as well as the fine gentlemen over there."

Such weakness in "leadership" could only show strength by destroying those who would not follow. Fascist leaders could only offer as a cause the crudity of imperial conquest and the defeat of the weak.

Today in peaceful "democratic" societies a parallel process is at work. Collectivist power and corporate patronage attract a professional core of politicians, paid for by the state and therefore adept at doing its will - and that will is to override the interests of free people. Such a structure can never attract democratic leaders, who would prefer the public good to the extraction of private profit from state power. For in such a system individuals, families and free associations responsibly pursuing their freedoms and offering unpaid aid to their neighbour, count for nothing. Only the collective counts - the corporation, the state, the interest group, the union, the industrial conglomerate, the bankers or any other interest which represents either numbers or power or lobbying muscle.

Such a system is tailor-made for the inadequate "leader", the politician without principle or ideas. Nothing is more dangerous to collectivist politics than a democratic leader with originality and moral strength. For such individuals may not "understand" where their interests lie! They may, like the free and responsible people who elected them, insist on their freedom of decision and an acceptance of responsibility to people in general rather than vested interests in particular.

So although such "leaders" may not seem aggressive or violent, their weakness allows corporate powers full reign to dominate through state violence. They are "placemen". By having no cause, ideas, principles or philosophy such opportunists must perpetually construct new majorities out of ever more incompatible minorities. In the United States what can unite, within President Clinton's Democratic party, socialists of Greek extraction with romantic Irish nationalists? - support for a terrorist organisation like the IRA which claims socialism and bombs the British. What could unite in "Europe" a Scottish trade unionist and a French farmer? - hatred of English landowners. What in John Major's Britain could unite country Conservatives and urban workers? - more police powers and identity cards to "stop crime". And what can unite warring Spanish and French fishermen? - a protectionist war against Canadian fishermen.

Such political mobilisation based on the lowest common denominator is common to 1930s dictatorships and present-day "multicultural", and multi-state "democracies" and would be the staple diet of a European superstate.

Equally important in the creation of political hatreds are the tensions created by the state's social and economic manipulations. As in the fascist era today's state still uses monetary manipulation to reduce its own debts through inflation - and thereby decimates the savings of the people. When they have thus impoverished generations of workers in their retirement, governments come to their "aid" with state subsidies - paid for out of ever higher taxes on the new generation of workers. And what has resulted from this merry-go-round? - more state patronage and less individual independence. Politicians still award grants and tax "incentives" to the large corporations and state enterprises which do not need them - paid for by those individuals, entrepreneurs and small businesses which cannot afford the bureaucratic infrastructure to apply for such state largesse - but who pay taxes to finance them.

In the United Kingdom, government has for generations spent tens of billions of pounds every year enticing savers and earners to direct their money towards banks, building societies and pension funds. Reliefs from high taxes were available **only if** individuals allowed their money to be thus collectivised into the City of London. Similarly the state itself, through nationalisation, inflation and high taxation, centralised economic and political decision making.

Where capital goes people must follow. And where capital becomes the plaything of politicians its distribution is not the result of public service of the many but of private lobbying of the few.

This collectivised and corporatised capital alienates the people and enhances the power of the state - a truly fascist process. Individuals are alienated from their families, families from their capital and regions from their businesses (the central state taxes the local business with local shareholders and subsidises the branch factory of the foreign corporation). Finally - as we witness in the "European Union" - even the nation and its loyalties are bargained away in a supranational political bazaar.

The remarkable aspect of modern politics in the United Kingdom is the fusion of the two main "opposing" political parties - Labour and Conservative. Both practise state subsidy, both believe in emasculating Parliament and surrendering national sovereignty, both are prepared to accept the abolition of the pound and the Bank of England, both believe in the professional politician and ever greater state payments to themselves and their parties, both believe in subsidising never-married mothers and families with two incomes (financed by married couples and single-income families), both believe in state and corporate power, ever higher government spending and taxes (the one says so - the other practises it). **If there is any socialism it is to be found in the massive interventions of a Conservative government and if there is any Conservatism it is to be found in the leader of the Labour Party.**

This is not surprising. This fusion of right and left, of socialism and capitalism, of unions and capital, of the state and the party, not to mention the power of the executive over Parliament and of the party over the MP - all this is the epitome of fascism and it is a process about which this author has been warning since the early 1980s.

Above all in Britain today weak leadership and lack of authority have led, as one would expect, to the ever more petulant and petty exercise of state power over free and responsible people.

The most remarkable attribute of the modern "democratic" state is the way in which politicians and governments cloak themselves in the trappings and privileges of the kind of absolute monarchy which democracy was supposed to replace. (No wonder the new "monarchy" wants to remove the established monarchy - a tyrant cannot allow others to wear his robes, even if their influence derives more from the people's allegiance than from true monarchical power). The government signed the Maastricht Treaty which took away the democratic rights of the British people, without consulting them and under "Crown Prerogative" - that is through the power of "the Crown" (i.e. the government) to effectively bypass Parliament.

When the British courts were, quite properly, asked to judge the legality of the Maastricht Treaty the Speaker of the House of Commons had the unmitigated gall to threaten the courts - the very upholders of the Rule of Law.

The government, which manages the National Health Service so incompetently, actually employed a detective agency to spy on consultants - to see how much of their time was spent on private patients. Similarly the "Highways Agency" (an arm of government masquerading as an independent entity) employed a detective agency to "monitor protesters at Twyford Down", the scene of anti-motorway demonstrations. Government (whose massive interventions and corporatist manipulations have alienated the people and brought about a crime wave) then erects cameras in the streets to spy on **everyone**. Needless to say even this state activity has now made common cause with corporatism through the sale of the film from these observation cameras to commercial interests who are selling the video recordings in retail outlets.

The recent trend of "floating off" civil service departments and encouraging state interests (like universities, schools and government offices) to compete against the private sector has led to increasing business failures among those who cannot call on the public purse for subsidy (or, like the state, create new laws to disadvantage their competitors).

Under the guise of "cutting red tape" the Government has introduced a Deregulation Bill which permits the removal of much historic legislation **without the need to ask for specific parliamentary approval**. As the excellent Christopher Booker has pointed out, while 21 innocuous laws have been repealed by the British Parliament 10,000 European Union directives have been introduced by Brussels.

The "privatisation" (in fact corporatisation) of former state monopolies has meant a proliferation of Regulatory Authorities which take on powers which even government cannot resist. A transport minister said he could only lay down guidelines for the rail regulator, he could not as the minister responsible for the railways, decide a minimum number of ticket offices.

There is no better example of economic fascism than the authorisation of agencies by the state to maximise their income or profits at the expense of a captive public. The Child Support Agency, intended as a means of making absent parents accept the costs of their children, soon became a profit-maximising effort for the state. An internal memo read *"The name of the game (sic) is maximising the yield. Don't waste time on the non profitable stuff"*. A better demonstration of the gulf between public service under direct public control and private benefit in a pseudo-privatised legal monopoly would be hard to find.

The Channel Tunnel is bankrupt - or rather the company which built it cannot pay its debts of some £8,000m. The banks who foolishly lent this vast sum, on the basis that it could not fail because it was launched, "backed" and opened by the British Prime Minister and the President of France, cannot even obtain interest due, never mind have their loans repaid. Times change and neither the British nor the French government is in a position to bail them out. The real tragedy however is that many private companies who did excellent work on the construction of the tunnel have lost monies due to them. One company which had been "persuaded and cajoled" to speed up its work to such an extent that contracts had been accepted without written instructions or guarantees, spent £9m but was forced to accept £7.15m in settlement. The only thing a corporatist state can guarantee is that the people, not the government, will pay for that guarantee. When the fanfares were blown to launch the tunnel, the governments and banks who threw away other people's money were prominent in the line-up of "dignitaries" - those who really built the project and lost their own money doing so will have no plaques to their names.

The essential element for a corporatist, fascist society is the combination of corporate capital and (absolute) state power. This operates equally efficiently at the local level. A Safeway supermarket was the subject of a planning application at Hexham in Northumberland. Public opinion (local traders and those who wished to preserve town centre shopping) was against the scheme, but the Director of Planning said "Public opinion had to be measured against other material considerations". It became clear what this other "material consideration" was - a bribe of £1m from the supermarket company to the council. This, in the words of the planning director was "... a material planning consideration which we were obliged to take into account." Such behaviour in any other walk of life would be seen as a bribe and those guilty would have been prosecuted. But in Britain today national government in London had decreed that this process acquired a legal, respectable name - "planning gain". This process has opened up the way all over the country for companies to bulldoze through planning applications - an excellent example of how the combination of corporatism and state power can override the wishes of people and communities.

John Major has been a master of corporatist manipulation of his own party. Having lost the support - and therefore the funds - of individual Conservatives, the party machine became increasingly reliant on large corporate donations. It was the reliance on supermarket donations which lead to the commercialisation of the Sabbath Day, a policy which would never have had the support of the Conservative party. Major therefore granted a "free vote" in Parliament and used the votes of Labour MPs to outvote opposition in his own party. (A similar process helped the passage of the Act lowering the homosexual age of consent, the law making divorce easier and, not least, the Maastricht Treaty legislation.)

The catastrophic destruction of the British constitution in the name of the "European Union" has equally been the result of corporatist lobbying of the Conservative party. The Confederation of British Industry pressed the Government first to shadow the ERM (massive inflation) then to join it (longest recession since the 1930s). The appalling policy record of the CBI - that arch representative of corporatist capital in Britain since the War - can be contrasted with the far better record of the Institute of Directors where the presence of real business owners and entrepreneurs (who are not perpetually going cap in hand to the nanny state) provides a breath of fresh, "free capitalist" air.

The network of state corporatist institutions has grown like Topsy - thanks to the activities of both Labour and Conservative governments. Their motivation was never to help the people and businessmen but to acquire more power over the business process which - to their chagrin - was already efficient, democratic and popular. Like OBEs for pop stars, Government interventions in economic and social systems are designed to raise the profile of politicians and allow *the people's* spontaneous success to rub off on the (largely despised) *state* apparatus.

One of the main engines of state corporatism has been the Enterprise Zone and the various "Development Agencies" which have given pompous titles to those who have failed to create wealth and jobs on their own account but believe they can do wonders with taxpayer's money.

The Enterprise Zones have been disastrous - taxing those many smaller companies *outside* to provide planning privileges and rate and rent holidays for the large (usually quoted) companies who set up *inside* the zone. The London Docklands Zone created no jobs for locals (who paid taxes to fund the subsidies) but enticed into Canary Wharf a major international developer who went bankrupt.

Up and down the country cases of corruption and misallocation of funds have been recorded in these state/corporatist, taxpayer-funded "enterprises". The Conservative government created these mixtures of socialism and capitalism and the Labour party have realised what a wonderful source of collectivist power they are. At a recent bye-election the Labour MP who won the seat previously held by Conservatives was the Chief Executive of a local "Enterprise Agency" funded by Conservative central government.

In another part of the country, Tameside Enterprise Development was a private company run and controlled by Labour politicians - set up in response to the Conservative government's push for private-sector tenders to run council services, in this case old people's homes. The owners of this "private" company were the council, a management "trust" and the local Labour Party. The positions of company director and secretary went to two Labour politicians and four other positions were held by close relations of Labour politicians.

Looking through Orwell's farmhouse window at today's Britain (and especially at the "European Union"), British voters see the worst aspects of both Conservative and Labour administrations. Both are engaged in the corporatist and covert corruptions which marginalise and exploit individuals, families and small businesses. Both parties are a threat to all free associations which lack the power to lobby, manipulate and feed off the power of the state. Indeed so corrupt has our parliament become that it is itself beholden to a foreign power which can ban our trade with the rest of the world, run our agriculture and fishing industries, outvote us in most policy areas and occasionally repatriate some of our own money if we do as we are told.

It is no wonder, as we gaze through Orwell's farm house window at politicians of all parties (costing us £250,000 a year each) that we can no longer distinguish between Tony Major, Paddy Blair and John Ashdown. No wonder that Parliament is ignored and its occupants despised. No wonder that all the freedoms for which we fought two world wars are disappearing as the plans laid by Eurofascism 60 years ago are daily imposed upon us.

(1) Anne Appelbaum recounting in *The Spectator* her own experiences as a potential candidate.

(2) Friedrich Reck-Malleczewen, Audiogrove, London, 1995, "Diary of a Man in Despair".

3

NATIONAL SOCIALIST INFLUENCE AFTER THE WAR

From 1925 until the mid-1970s fascist government enjoyed extraordinary political power in Europe. Although the period between 1933 and 1945 when Hitler, Mussolini and Franco dominated Europe was its heyday, it was not until Spain achieved democracy in the 1980s that the fascist era was over. Or rather it seemed to be over. In fact as we have seen in other chapters the true essence of a fascist society is in its *social and economic* structures and those ideas have even infiltrated those countries which were not ruled by fascist governments. Today those ideas and structures have been faithfully reproduced in the European Union. How did that come about?

It was always a naive belief that a political and economic system which conquered virtually the whole of Europe and came within a hair's breadth of overrunning the Soviet Union would suddenly and without protest fold its tents in 1945 and disappear into the dust of history. The belief that this did happen was nevertheless widespread and was made more credible by the association of the German and Italian fascist systems with extravagant and demonised leaders who met their deaths at the end of the war.

In fact after the war two centres of Nazi theory and political influence were established - in Stuttgart (the Evangelical Relief Organisation) and Madrid (the so-called "Girozentrale"). The latter issued frequent "circular letters", two of which in 1950 expressed the opinions:

> "Germany as the exponent of European neutrality could gain far reaching concessions from the Soviets." (1)

and

> "The so-called American democracy does not deserve the sacrifice of the bones of a single German soldier ... what Germany needs in the future is not democracy but a system of statecraft similar to that of the Soviet dictatorship which would enable the political and military elite in Germany to organise the industrial capacity of Europe and the military qualities of the German people for the revival of the German race and the re-establishment of Europe as the power centre of the world."

Certainly the modern Eurostate has been created without reference to anything as sordid as democracy, German power over its neighbours has not been so great since 1943 and "European" Commissioners seek a world role for their fledgling superstate. Indeed through a world-wide spread of "European Union ambassadors" they are well on the way to achieving it.

Heinrich Hauser, in a book published in the USA at the end of the war, *The German Talks Back*, did not mince his words in perpetuating Nazi ideas:

> "Germans are disgusted with western civilisation, the culmination of which was and is the United States."

But more dangerous than the fringe Nazi elements active after the Second World War was the influence of former Nazis in the post-war German government and the influence of leading Nazis like Albert Speer whose volte face from fanatical Nazi leader (in charge of all Nazi war production) to post-war appeaser of and adviser to leading Americans, had undue influence on the shape of Europe.

Speer had been responsible with his French Vichyite colleague Jean Bichelonne for the "Franco-German Production Council", one of whose achievements was the transfer of consumer goods production from Germany to France in order to stop the leakage of labour to the underground. Speer's post-war interrogation by, among others, George Ball, Kenneth Galbraith and Paul Nitze, in which he pushed for a Europe based on his economic system, led to just such a creation. Ball and Nitze were *rapporteurs* at the first Bilderberg meeting, the former writing in his book *The Discipline of Power* (!).

> "We must persist in encouraging the building of a unified western Europe as we have sought to do since the war."

It was of course George Ball's influence on Kennedy and Johnson which bounced the naive Harold Macmillan into his betrayal of the British Commonwealth and his appointment of Edward Heath as the chief negotiator on the UK's entry into the EEC.

Speer also made contact with John McCloy who was Chairman of the Allied High Commission in Berlin and later Chairman of the Chase Manhattan Bank - the family bank of the Rockefellers who have ever since sustained the American pillar of Bilderberg. Albert Speer so ingratiated himself with his interrogators that he was sentenced to prison rather than death (unlike his deputy, Sauckel).

It is therefore not surprising that the long-term power game of Hitler's Germany (well described in *Mein Kampf*) was alive and well in the "democratic" Germany and the embryo Europe of the early 50s (when the European Coal and Steel Community was based entirely on Speer's Franco-German industrial model).

In the early 50s the newspaper *Der Fortschritt* in Essen discussed the geopolitical meaning for Germany of any Western European economic system:

> "While integration with the West restricts our industry to markets where we are subjected to cut throat competition, the Eastern block offers us markets where countless millions are hungry for our industrial goods."

The important thing for Germany then as now was to tie down its competitors in the West and ruthlessly exploit the East - a plan now made conveniently easy by the British Foreign Office and its attempt to hold back EU *integration* by seeking EU *expansion* into Eastern Europe. Germany has already built up the former East Germany with billions of pounds of industrial subsidies from the European Union (much of it paid for by British taxpayers). It anticipates a similar process further east.

The aim of colonising Africa, using "Europe" as the front for German interests was reflected in Adenauer's speeches, in the German press and in post-war Nazi organs in the USA. Adenauer is quoted by Henry Brandon the *Sunday Times* correspondent in the USA, in his book *The Retreat of American Power*:

> "Look at Europe - what does it consist of? Britain? - aloof. France? - politically unstable ... Italy? - economically unstable. And Benelux doesn't count. What does Europe therefore consist of? - Germany."

The newspaper *Christ und Welt* in Stuttgart could dress up Germany's ambitions in the cloak of "Europe" in 1951:

> "A united Europe possessing its own powerful army could begin the development of its colonial empire in Africa."

In the December 1944 issue of "Neue Volkszeitung" in New York Friedrich Stampfer wrote of the prospective results of a German-Russian pact:

> "... the final destruction of the French-British barrier, the liquidation of the British Empire and the end of West European colonial rule. This would mean the establishment of German domination over Africa."

Today, where once British aid and investment was welcomed in our former colonies, the "European Union" marches in to Africa with its "help", its propaganda and its flag - mostly financed by the annual British budget contribution to Brussels of £7,500 million (rising to £10,000m by 1997).

The Madrid *Geopolitical Centre* continued its mission in the early 1950s, realising (like Hitler) that the authoritarian nature of the Roman Catholic Church was a vital ingredient in the creation of a new non-democratic Europe. Like Helmut Kohl with his "fate", the Nazis realised the power of "mystical elements":

> "Democracy is a wishy washy term which has found no ear among the German people. The mystical element and the religious tradition embodied in the concept of the Reich sparks our political mission and is especially attractive within the Catholic world."

The Centre saw the German and Vatican interests as identical if the USA and the USSR should be weakened in a protracted struggle. Their ideas echo modern-day Germany's extraordinary hatred of the Serbs:

> "It is entirely to the interest of the Roman Catholic Church to see to it that the (schismatic) orthodox Slavs ("Schismatisches Slaventum") and the predominant Protestant North American continent must be weakened for a long time to come."

These extreme Nazi ideas were indeed influential and were picked up by the establishment press in Germany. In 1952 the *Frankfurter Allgemeine*, echoing Hitler's 1939 Molotov-Ribbentrop pact:

> "In order to jump out of her present isolation Russia can, exactly as the Rappallo Treaty did 30 years ago, place Germany as a protecting buffer between East and West ... she could repeat the old game for world position by concluding long-term agreements with German industry."

This kind of German threat, taken seriously, would have forced the Allies to change tack after the war had they not already decided to do so because of the Soviet communist threat, the Berlin airlift and the ideas of one George Kennan, the principal US State Department theoretician on post-war Europe. Kennan's new approach rejected the initial Roosevelt policy of strict control of German power and instead recommended the building of German industrial and military power as a counterbalance to and a "containment" of Russian power. This was of course similar to the policy which the Nazis had pursued and which their post-war apologists were recommending.

The risks involved can be seen in the attitudes of even "moderate" German politicians and journalists. The *Frankfurter Allgemeine* of July 17th 1951:

> "... all concessions in the direction of German equality were won only after Germany had exercised relentless pressure. According to François Poncet well behaved children do not cry - but well behaved children will never get anything ..."

Adenauer's regime aimed (as Hitler had done) to use the Russian threat to emphasise the need for a "united Europe" and use that concept to justify firstly the re-unification of Germany and then the re-acquisition of former German territories. Jacob Kaiser, Adenauer's "Minister for Unification" in the early 1950s:

> "No real Europe can be formed until the German block is reconstructed. I remind you that this block includes in addition to Germany, Austria and a part of Switzerland, the Saar and Alsace Lorraine. When I think of Strasbourg Cathedral my heart hurts."

With this disturbing background the plan to revitalise Germany as a bulwark against Russian communism (even by anyone other than Kennan) could be seen as a risky enough strategy but perhaps acceptable in the face of a greater risk of Europe being overrun by the Russian army. *But Kennan's background was controversial.* He had studied German geopolitics in Heidelberg and Berlin and took up a post in the American embassy in Germany when, due to the entry of the USA into the war, he was interned for a time at Bad Nauheim. There, according to post-war reports in the German magazine *Der Spiegel*, Kennan lectured with the Nazi regime's approval on geopolitics - propounding views sympathetic to the Nazi cause. He claimed that Germany's defeat:

> "would extinguish the 2,000-year-old history of European civilisation."

and blamed the West which, had it adopted a less forceful policy, could have:

> "enforced a greater circumspection on the Nazi regime and cause it to proceed more slowly with the actualisation of its timetable." (2)

Kennan's propensity to appease the power of anti-democractic regimes continued throughout his life and in particular in his later attitude to the Soviet Union. He spoke of Lenin's "fundamental idealism" and his "reluctance and heaviness of heart that he was obliged to concede the necessity of terror". (3)

Kennan even had difficulty in distinguishing between the Soviet tyranny and American democracy: (4)

> "As for the one party system (in Russia)...In the doctrinal sense we in America also have in certain respects a one party system. For aren't the two parties ideologically indistinguishable?"

As ambassador in Russia he talked of that country's "general beneficence of nature and human sociability" and contrasted it with New York which was "today unfit for civilised living". He even recommended a "relaxed and sympathetic tolerance for normal authoritarianism" and propounded an elitism which Nazi Germany would have admired, recommending: (5)

> "...some detached and austere authority such as the Supreme Court (which) could then say to the electorate 'You can nominate people for election to the Senate but only from this body'."

Whereas Hitler, following General Haushofer's geopolitical theory, built German military might to first neutralise and then conquer Western and Eastern Europe, George Kennan's new Pentagon policy built up German military and economic power to contain Russia and proposed a united Europe in which Germany would become the principal force. In Hitler's case the Germans would pay, while in Kennan's plan NATO would pay for military power and the European Community would help to finance Germany's economic resurrection.

So long as Germany was not united and NATO remained the power within which Germany was bound, and so long as the European Union remained an *economic* vehicle for post-war prosperity, then Kennan's plan might be excused as the best of a bad choice. But today, while the Bilderberger Kennan's plan remains intact, the conditions have changed out of all recognition. Germany is re-united, it is by far the most powerful economy in Europe, its population size means that the increasingly political nature of the European Union gives it unparallelled power and its leaders are showing extraordinary aggression in their plans to "integrate" the nations of Europe (which Kennan's Pentagon had fought in two wars to free from German tyranny). Germany consistently promotes its own nationalist interests while condemning other European countries as "nationalist". Germany bullied its partners into locating the European Central Bank in Frankfurt and insists (under the guise of anti-inflationary sentiments among Germans) that a Euro-currency must be a *de facto* German currency. Helmut Kohl even warns (or threatens) the possibility of war if Germany does not get its way.

Perhaps this is what Kennan meant by allowing Germany to "proceed with the actualisation of its timetable"! Commenting on the apparent need to "strengthen" post-war Germany, Walter Lippman wrote in 1947 in the *Herald Tribune*:

> "For the Germans to whom the mastery of the Continent is the supreme goal, the war would not have been fought in vain. If thirty years hence Germany dominates Europe and thus holds the balance of power between Russia and the English speaking nations, German historians will not count this war as a true defeat."

So the Nazis have come again, initially in their social and economic forms, increasingly in their political policies and attitudes and supported (see Chapter 7) by the same kind of people and corporations which were so helpful in the 1930s and 1940s. Few understand how or why a tyrant cannot be recognised by his tyrannical behaviour (until it is too late). In fact tyrants usually arrive with gifts and the new Eurostate is no exception, except of course that those gifts have already been paid for by the British taxpayer in his massive contributions to the EU budget. (Even Hitler paid for his conquest of other nations with Germany's own money!)

Today those gifts come in the form of maternity leave, pension rights, "European grants" to industry and farming subsidies. But just as the social chapter, sold as "protection" of British labour, turns out to be the protection of German labour from British competition, so these other gifts are not just undemocratic (imposed on an elected British government against its will) and destructive of jobs but more significantly they represent an unrivalled opportunity for the Eurostate to propagandise in our country and insist on the display of its imperialist flag in our land. Will the new people of Troy ever awaken to the danger?

(1) This and other quotations in this chapter are from T. H. Tetens "Germany plots with the Kremlin".

(2) See Tetens who reports his conversation with the then editor of *Der Spiegel*.

(3) *Encounters with Kennan*, Frank Cass, London, 1979, page 208.

(4) ibid page 212

(5) ibid page 214

4

THE EUROPEAN UNION AND THE 1942 NAZI PLANS FOR EUROPE

In the introduction to the book *Die Europäishe Wirtschaftsgemeinschaft*, published in Berlin in 1942 the leading Nazi academic Professor Heinrich Hunke, expressed ideas which have recently found favour with the present leader of Germany, Chancellor Helmut Kohl. (1)

> "The Anglo Saxon economic system, the classic national economy, is dead."

Again, echoing almost identical words by Helmut Kohl in the 1990s Hunke, lapsing into the dangerous deterministic romanticism of Nazi Germany, wrote in 1942 of:

> "The community of fate which is the European economy."

and:

> "The continent is, with Germany and Italy, bound by fate."

The dangerous notion that individuals and states are driven by "fate" is reflected in today's Europe in the frequent use of the words "irrevocable" and "irreversible" in the Maastricht Treaty. Those obsessed by "fate" are the first to be obsessed by methods of political and economic control - to ensure that their idea of "fate" actually comes about. They are also those who easily resort to threats when they do not seem to be getting their own way. Despite the fact that the European Community was built on the Franco-German axis and the apparent friendship between Adenauer and de Gaulle, Schmidt and Giscard d'Estaing, and Kohl and Mitterand, the slightest hint of

France not going along with Germany's idea of "fate" is met by an extraordinary aggression. Germany's ruling CDU/CSU recently issued a threatening document:

> "If Germany puts forward clear and unequivocal proposals then France must make equally clear and unequivocal decisions ... France must rectify the impression that, although it allows no doubt as to its basic will to pursue integration, it often hesitates in taking concrete steps towards this objective."

With "friends" like this, no wonder Chirac is cooperating in more joint military projects with the United Kingdom.

Like those who, since the Second World War, and in particular since the fall of the Soviet block, have talked of the "new world order" and the "modern" importance of supranational power blocks, so the Nazi Hunke was convinced 55 years ago that:

> "The monocultures are a result of that economic theory which sees in the world market price the determining factor of the economy. Europe is in the best position to destroy these monocultures."

In other words the free nations based for the most part on such "monocultures" and the free interaction between them in the form of free trade and market prices (i.e. freely, not collectively, determined) must be swept aside and replaced by collectivism. The free nation was to be replaced by the omniscient, powerful state which would reject free movement of capital and market prices and replace them with the power of labour, represented politically by the new "national socialism". The power of the new Europe would set centrally the price of goods and labour and "organise" the economic system to fit the political will. To quote Hunke in the full flow of that same interventionism which characterises the modern European Union:

> "There can be no doubt that the idea of the controlled economy or rather leading the economy, is revolutionary ... it means the final decision in all questions of economic

power are made by the state ... and the solidarity of the individual national economies"

He believed, just as Delors, Mitterand, Kohl and the modern "builders of Europe" believe today that:

"the fate and extent of European cooperation depend on a new unitary economic plan."

No wonder that Hunke was well aware of the opposition to these ideas by the British - and the entire Anglo Saxon world which, in fascist Europe, became the object of such contempt and (as the great **Continental economic system** fell apart) hatred. Writing in 1942, when Hitler had lost any hope of coming to an accommodation with the British appeasers (whose literal and intellectual descendants dominate the Eurofanatic establishment today) Hunke realised how Britain was inherently opposed to the Nazi agenda.

"The prospects and scope of European economic unity however remained problematic so long as the Fuhrer could hope that an accommodation with England was possible."

Those who today claim that only by being inside the European Union can "the wrong kind of Europe" be prevented should consider that it was only after Britain's declaration of war (and the internal defeat of the advocates of appeasement) that a process began which ended in the defeat of corporatist/fascist Europe.

The principal author and architect of the ideas contained in *"Die Europäische Wirtschaftsgemeinschaft"* was Walther Funk. His contribution to the book begins with the claim that because Britain dominated world trade, industry and finance and even fulfilled the role of world policeman, the European countries did not benefit from the world's wealth creation. With Hitler, Funk claimed that Germany could right this injustice. Free trade and market prices had created the "British capitalist era" and (with an eye to the resentment of the European peasant farmer) he concluded:

"Agriculture could not benefit in the face of the interests of industry, trade, banking and stock exchange."

It is important to recall that during the terrible inflation in 1920s Germany those with land enjoyed lavish offers of debt finance from the banks (as in Britain and the USA in the 1970s). The financial collapse and subsequent recession and deflation bankrupted thousands of peasant farmers who became supporters of the Nazi party. The repeat of this *inflation - debt - deflation - bankruptcy* cycle in the 1980s and 1990s in Europe and the USA is, just as in Germany in the 1920s and 1930s, leading to a dangerous alienation of voters from mainstream political parties - those powers which are (rightly) seen as responsible for leading the gullible masses into such a financial trap.

Fascism's large debt to socialist theory and rhetoric, not to mention state socialist forms of power, is denied to this day by "the left" but the class-based hatreds of the worker and peasant farmer were well exploited by the Nazis, French Vichy and Italian Fascists. (Jacques Delors, a former member of the Vichyite youth movement, the *Compagnons de France*, made a similar pitch for the support of British industrial workers when he addressed the Trade Union Congress on the glories of the new Eurostate.)

Of course communism was as much an enemy of fascism as of capitalism but fascism saw communism as its rival for the affections of the masses and therefore used similar methods to recruit them. Indeed many young men and women in the 1930s in Germany used to turn out to demonstrate for the Nazis in the morning and for the communists in the afternoon - marchers being modestly remunerated by both factions!

Funk and the Nazis saw the emancipation of the landed and urban worker in:

"... freeing the economy from international financial interests and dependence on economic fluctuations and the voluntary subordination of the individual to the primacy of the national economy."

The inevitable failures of collectivism always lead to more extreme forms of collectivism. The social democrat and conservative interventionist economics of Weimar Germany led inevitably to the totalitarian controls imposed by 1930s' fascism. The very state which had underwritten the inflation and collectivism of "social" or "Christian" democracy was the first to claim (under new leadership) that only the state could rescue the people from the consequences. Large corporations, who had also benefited from inflation, were able, unlike small farmers, to balance the new deflation with increased exports, encouraged by those foreign countries and bankers who looked to such earnings to fund their vast loans to Germany (originally granted to finance reparations after the First World War).

Needless to say, "freeing the economy from financial interests" means establishing the power of the state and state-organised corporations over savers, investors and consumers. This is the essence of socio-economic fascism and its corporatist structures - putting the collective above the individual, the corporation above the investor and the producer above the consumer. Such policies lead always and everywhere to the political and economic suppression of individuals, families, entrepreneurs and small businesses.

This leads inevitably to what I call the **"imperial necessity of collectivism"** - that is the inexorable logic of extending the control and organisation of individuals and communities to the control of corporations and nations. From there (in order to prevent free competition from nations not so controlled) *groups* of nations must be controlled - in line with Hunke's "solidarity of individual national economies".

Such international "block" collectivism leads to the perceived need to own and exploit (by owning, not by trading) the basic commodities in nations further afield. Funk boasted in 1942:

> "Even today a large, indeed the most valuable part of Soviet Russia's territory is under our control and we are concentrating our energies on opening up this massive source of raw materials"

For the logic of the socialist, communist or fascist must be to extend the "needs" of society beyond the boundaries of the societies and nations they wish to destroy. Funk again:

> "No nation in Europe can achieve on its own the highest level of economic freedom which is compatible with all social requirements."

We see the exact same logic in today's Eurofanatics who pour scorn on "national sovereignty" and promote instead the need for "power" to "compete in world markets" - even though the most successful global competitors are nation states like Germany, Japan and the USA and the most unstable have proved to be federal systems like the Soviet Union and Yugoslavia. And of course it is the nation states, not the superstates, which have provided the most advanced systems of social support (Bismark's Germany and post war Britain being good examples). The controlling, imperialist ambitions of the politician are often dressed up in words like "freedom", "competition" and "social services" when the actual plan would lead to the opposite as they try to impose political systems which will control these "freedoms".

The perpetual logic of the collectivist, be he socialist, communist or fascist, is that where there is inherent conflict then the conflicting parties must be abolished. For instance the socialist sees the end of class conflict in the abolition of the classes. The liberal by contrast finds ever more free, responsible, contract-based systems of economic trade, financial relations and democratic accountability between competing interests, communities and nations. The collectivist, because he seeks to control and protect, always sees those outside his system of control either as the enemy or as a potential part of a greater whole (which he will control). The Nazi Funk sums up this "lager" mentality:

> "(east and west Europe) can feed and clothe itself and provide all the goods required ... the European economic area will in future be resistant to blockades ... then economic wars will no longer make any sense."

The next step, Funk concludes, is obvious:

> "The formation of very large economic areas follows a natural law of development."

while his view of the riches of Africa is not based on free trade but on the control of colonies:

> "In addition we will have at our disposal from the colonies in the tropical zones of Africa all the luxuries which make life pleasant ..."

The process by which the logic of socio-economic control leads automatically to the control of other nations and then the acquisition of an empire can be seen in these further ideas of Walther Funk, the Nazis' leading economic theorist:

> "state economic control and inter-state agreements in Europe will control the acquisition of raw materials, the regulation of production, sales and the use of labour."

> "the Rumanian peasant, the Norwegian timber merchant, the Dutch gardener and the Danish poultry producer need not worry that they will not be able to sell their produce or not receive a good price. They will know that production and sale through inter-governmental contracts are assured."

Of course the Nazis did not have the expensive and corrupt failure of the European Common Agricultural Policy to serve as an example, otherwise they would have known that state support always leads to state control and then to state destruction, not just of domestic but also of overseas markets. The CAP now pays rich farmers to grow nothing, pays peasants for vineyards and olive trees which do not exist and bankrupts farmers with bureaucracy. Third world markets are destroyed as Euro-state boosted surpluses are dumped abroad (the Mafia taking its cut!). There is nothing more corrupt than state control, sold to a gullible public as "security".

There was no doubt in the minds of leading Nazi, fascist and Vichyite economists that the enemy of this closed system of economic control was the Anglo Saxon trading system. While Funk maintains that Germany had "nothing against a healthy trade with overseas states" (note the term "overseas" - i.e. far enough away from fortress Europe to escape control of the "economic area"!) he nevertheless rejects:

> "a world economy of the old style which is dependent on an overt or disguised Anglo-American world dominance. It is precisely because we want to prevent that that we are constructing a European economic block"

All free political systems are based on free economic systems in which capital and the returns to capital cannot be dictated by those who own it. If the state, which has absolute power, involves itself in the control of capital then labour in general will not receive its value and consumers will not have the freedom to control the excesses of capital. It is the mobility of capital which spreads wealth around the world and makes it unnecessary for large migrations from poor nations to rich. Only free capital can provide an alternative to the potentially oppressive power of the state or corporate monopolies.

But such openness and freedom cannot be tolerated by dictatorships and hence Hitler's attack on Anglo-Saxon capitalism and its international freedom. Similarly the domestic equivalents (individual or family capital or entrepreneurial wealth and small and medium-sized businesses) could not be tolerated. The populist corporatist solution was to "replace capital with labour". As Hitler himself preached:

> "We speak not of capital but of labour and that labour we employ to 100% effect."

Like socialists everywhere who talk of the power of labour, the Nazis meant of course that the state would represent labour and make decisions on labour's behalf. So the powerlessness of capital, far from emancipating the people, would produce more scope for the absolute power of the state.

Since the Nazi regime did not recognise market forces and prices set by free trade in the *international* sphere, a similar attitude prevailed *domestically*. As one would expect, given the combination of conservative interventionism and socialist controls, this regime resembled the British governments run by Labour and Heathite Conservatives between 1964 and 1979. The stability of the currency (the Reichsmark) was considered to require state controls of prices, wages and foreign exchange. In his contribution to *"Die Europäische Wirtschaftsgemeinschaft"* Dr Bernhard Benning, director of the *Reichs-Kredit-Gesellschaft* in Berlin, praises the success of such controls in "controlling inflation". Of course inflation cannot be defeated by any government control of *symptoms* because government (and those whom government empowers) is itself the ultimate *cause* of inflation. The *proximate* cause is of course monetary expansion or "money printing".

But this interventionist, often called "social", economic engineering predominates in today's European Union where such procrustean ideas lead to the desire to control those very prices which might indicate the failure of this philosophy - exchange rates. As the Nazi Benning put it in 1942:

> "... price stability in the partner countries (of Europe) will permit less friction in the currency relations between European countries."

"Price stability" or the absence of inflation does not in itself lead to stability in exchange rates since the latter are also affected by balance of payments deficits and surpluses and capital movements - regardless of levels of inflation.

Once again we see the attempt to eliminate "friction" rather than to accomodate it as a natural symptom of economic and international interaction. Note also the word "stability", so often heard from national corporatists like the Confederation of British Industry and supranational corporatists like the European Commission. They want to fix prices, exchange rates and interest rates - indeed any free signal of supply, demand, success or failure. At least they do until the full hideous consequences of this philosophy hit those who have recommended it! The CBI *now* regrets the farcical attempts to "shadow the Deutschmark" (which produced high inflation followed by high interest rates) and entry into the European

Exchange Rate Mechanism (which caused the longest recession since the 1930s) - but they were eager supporters of both in the name of "stability".

The ERM's attempt to remove friction from European currency movements had its exact equivalent in Benning's Europe of the 1940s:

> "We have succeeded, through the effective control of the economy, and in particular through price controls, in holding the currency stable."

This had allowed:

> "... a harmonious cooperation between governmental and business forces."

Needless to say, the Nazis' price controls imposed since 1936 had not stopped prices rising out of control in other Continental countries - indeed just as today the attempt to impose discipline through the ERM has caused massive devaluations of other currencies against the Deutschmark, so Germany's neighbours under the Nazis suffered from Germany's "controls".

Cumulative inflation between 1939 and 1942

Sweden	61%	Hungary	59%
Denmark	89%	Bulgaria	66%
Switzerland	85%	Rumania	145%(to mid-1941)

The national or international economy is like a balloon - an attempt to hold in one side will merely put more pressure on another until repeated attempts to "control" the balloon lead to an explosion, shocking the "controller".

An example of how the desire to dictate market forces when they do not produce what the dictator desires, and how that economic intervention leads to political aggression, is clear from another contributor to *"Die Europäische Wirtschaftsgemeinschaft"*, Gustav Koenig, an official in the German government in Berlin:

"Germany can no longer do without iron ore, Scandinavia can no longer do without coal and foreign shipping capacity, especially tramp shipping is not available because they are taken up by England. Free market forces are failing and a new system must be found ... We have a real European Community task before us ... and I am convinced that this Community effort will last beyond the end of the war."

The European Community was therefore intended by the Nazis (whose concept is the basis of today's European Union) as a common cause against British and Anglo-Saxon economic systems of trade and free exchange. Certainly that has been the result.

Few leading European Union politicians dare say in public what they believe in private but such anti-Anglo-Saxon attitudes are never far below the surface. During the crisis caused by the French government's nuclear tests in the South Pacific, *Le Figaro* decided that public opinion was being manipulated by "Anglo Saxon capitalist imperialism" (and rather spoiled this approach by describing France's "rightful place in the South Pacific"). In a recent French book taken seriously by Jacques Delors, the author, Alain Minc, a typical product of French state corporatist institutions, claims there is no future for *"le libre-echangisme anglo saxon"* for such ideas *"are not a philosophy, still less a programme for order."*

Corporatist elements in the present European Union seek to extend their protectionism using the same language. Philippe Maystadt, the Belgian Finance Minister recently said it was important to establish a single currency "core" in order to stand firm *"against Anglo-Saxon values"*. Both French and Belgian governmental circles are proposing that even those countries who stay outside a single currency must be controlled by the EU monetary authorities. As Alain Juppé, the French Prime Minister, said of those EU countries not joining a single currency:

"A single market cannot work if the Euro co-exists with currencies subject to competitive devaluation."

A better example of the "imperial necessity of collectivism" is hard to imagine. As the author frequently pointed out to British ministers from 1985 onwards, the very term "a single market" is an economic contradiction in terms and could only be understood as a political construction designed to create a Euro-state.

But such a concept, and the French, German and European socio-economic structures based upon it, are already failing as the massive increase in European Union unemployment contrasts with successful job creation in the USA, Britain and South East Asia, all economies firmly based on the wicked *"libre-echangisme anglo saxon"*.

The United Kingdom has today a trading surplus with every continent in the world except Europe. This is precisely why our social, economic and political entanglement within the new Eurostate is so attractive to our corporatist enemies in the European Union (just as it was to the Nazis). It is rather less obvious as to why this idea should appeal to British politicians.

(1) This and other quotations in this chapter are from *Die Europäische Wirtschaftsgemeinschaft* by Walther Funk, Nazi Minister of Economics, and others, Berlin, 1942.

5

ARNOLD TOYNBEE AND THE ATTACK ON THE NATION STATE

As I point out in Chapter 7, the Royal Institute of International Affairs based at Chatham House, St James's Square, London was founded by those corporate interests most active in supranational bodies, devoted to the weakening and elimination of the nation state and involved in activities which helped to sustain the Nazi government and the efficacy of its war machine.

In this chapter I will analyse a paper presented at the 1931 "Fourth Conference of Institutions for the Scientific Study of International Relations" by Arnold Toynbee, from 1925 to 1955 the Director of Studies at Chatham House. His 12-volume *A Study of History* was published by Oxford University Press between 1934 and 1961. He spent the years of the First World War working in the Political Intelligence Department of the Foreign Office and the Second World War in the Foreign Office Research Department. He was a Reith lecturer in 1952 and was made a Companion of Honour in 1956.

It is therefore not surprising that, given Toynbee's unrivalled Establishment credentials, the Royal Institute of International Affairs should be so coy in revealing his absurd, outlandish and violent denunciations of the nation state from which he received such honours (he was also made a *membre associé de l'Institut de France* in 1968). When I wrote to Chatham House to request a copy of the paper delivered at the 1931 conference *The Trend of International Affairs since The War*, I was sent only a summary (despite having paid in advance for the photocopying of the whole paper). When I eventually persuaded the Institute to send me the full paper, it became obvious why the 13-page "Summary" had been sent rather than the full, extraordinary paper itself. For this reveals Toynbee as the wild, aggressive, nation hating, world government fanatic which his *Dictionary of National Biography* entry does not quite encapsulate in the phrase "Toynbee was a quiet, charming, courteous and kindly man".

I will begin with the parts of the paper deliberately omitted from the "Summary". Toynbee, like most world government fanatics, sees the world based on democratic nations as "anarchy". One of the means of overcoming this "problem" is to use the excuse of disarmament to coerce the nations into giving up their sovereignty:

> "... if the first World Disarmament Conference does not achieve its purpose we shall call a second and a third ... we shall persist until we have not only solved the special problem of national armaments but the general problem of international anarchy of which armaments are a symptom."

It was of course just such arguments that President Kennedy embraced when he seriously considered the ludicrous notion that the way to prevent nuclear war was for the USA and USSR to surrender their nuclear arsenals to the United Nations. Like most of the superficial arguments of statists, interventionists and believers in world government, it is always the symptom of a problem which is attacked, never its cause. The major cause of the wars of the 20th century has been the fascist, communist or imperialist desires to eliminate the nation state. That Toynbee, who shared this aim, or any of the supranational institutions which he proposed, could conceivably be seen as peace makers is of course laughable. Supreme power, organised by supranational collectivists, is the greatest danger facing the world, the most insidious aspect of that philosophy being the power (and the will) to exclude any competitive challenge or competitive truths - for all alternatives are a danger to such hegemony. It is of course just those who propose the elimination of the free trading nation state who are most adept at domestic legislation which gives state control over the individual, family and autonomous communities. For it is these structures which form the basis of that organic, free hierarchy of which the nation is the largest sustainable unit to which allegiance can realistically be given.

In his paper Toynbee realises the public unacceptability of his vision:

> "If we are frank with ourselves we shall admit that we are engaged in a deliberate and sustained and concentrated effort to impose limitations upon the sovereignty and the independence of the fifty or sixty local sovereign independent States which at present ... divide the political allegiance of mankind."

Of course under the control of supranationalists like Toynbee there would be no "division" - just simple rule by his own elite. In this arrogant pursuit of the destruction of national democracies Toynbee admits the necessary conspiracy: (There is a horrific honesty which the true fanatic shows when he feels he is among a narrow group of friends.)

> "It is just because we are really attacking the principle of local sovereignty that we keep on protesting our loyalty to it so loudly. The harder we press our attack upon the idol, the more pains we take to keep its priests and devotees in a fool's paradise - lapped in a false sense of security which will inhibit them from taking up arms in their idols' defence."

If, as Toynbee claims, national sovereignty is a "false God" then it may be wondered why it is necessary to be so vicious, secretive and devious in attacking it. Partly perhaps because he fears it is too powerful and partly because he revels in his conspiracy:

> "... we are at present working discreetly but with all our might to wrest this mysterious political force called sovereignty out of the clutches of the local nation states of

> the world. And all the time we are denying with our lips what we are doing with our hands."

But Toynbee shows true confidence that "the monster is doomed to perish by our sword". Here speaks the true fascist - he who uses violence and believes in "doom". How redolent of Hitler's (and Helmut Kohl's) "fate" which is seen as more powerful than the allegiance of man to a nation. But just in case fate isn't quite so invincible the fanatic will have his sword to hand!

For just as Jacques Delors predicted the demise of the nation in the foundation of the European Union, and just as the Nazis saw France and England surviving merely as names (see chapter 9), so Toynbee echoed in the early 1930s the fascist agenda:

> "(the nations) will no doubt survive as administrative conveniences but sovereignty will depart from them ... it will cease in fact if not in name to be a local affair."

And anticipating the foolish (or perhaps worse) John Major when he saw for centuries to come old ladies cycling to church and warm beer served in the pub, and Kenneth Clarke claiming that the Queen's head will appear on the British version of the "Euro" coin:

> "For a local state may lose its sovereignty without losing those familiar features which endear it to the local patriot - vernacular language, folk lore, monuments. So long as the local state is not stripped of these harmless trappings it will remain almost as effective an idol as ever."

Once again the arrogance of the fascist shows through - beer and skittles for the stupid masses, power for the new elite in their "wisdom". Toynbee is well aware of the power of national and religious allegiance and like the Nazis with their Nordic gods and often satanic symbolism this "academic" aims to replace the religion of the nations with his own "divinity":

> "The local national state, invested with the attributes of sovereignty - invested that is with the prestige and the

> prerogatives of the medieval Church - is an abomination of desolation standing in a place where it ought not ... our political task ... is *to cast the abomination out, to cleanse the temple and to restore the worship of the divinity to whom the temple rightly belongs* ... to some institution embodying our society as a whole. In the world as it is today, this institution can hardly be a universal Church." (my emphasis)

Note that this embryo Hitler wants to replace the divinity in the temple with his own mystic power - because like all true fascists he knows the mesmeric effect of such powers on the masses he will control. Both communist and fascist systems replaced Christian religious services with their own quasi-religious political "initiations". During the rule of the communist regime in East Germany a youth initiation into the adult world, "Die Jugendweihe", was designed to mimic and replace the Christian confirmation. But it was based on the Nazi (pagan based) coming-of-age ritual. Both types of regime used the ceremonies to induct and demand allegiance of impressionable youth to the political system and ideological "bible" of their respective tyrannies.

So much then for those parts of Toynbee's 1931 speech which the Royal Institute of International Affairs omitted from the "summary" sent to me.

Why is it that we don't hear this kind of language today? Does it mean that no one thinks or plans these preposterous fantasies? No, it does not - for now they are actually realising these notions in the political power structures of "Europe" and the embryo "world order". (1) But now there are inquisitive writers and journalists, more open government (although the Conservative Government did not publish the Maastricht Treaty until after the election they claimed approved it!) and far more circumspect academics. The masses are not so deferential as in 1931 when the Toynbees of this world could plot the betrayal of their country as the drums of euro-fascism began to roll. At that time the pseudo-intellectual Oxbridge political analyst with ambitions to rule the world could enjoy his plotting coteries without fear of exposure.

But even today attempts are made by the Royal (sic) Institute of International Affairs to hide all the rabid power-crazed nonsense quoted above. And no wonder, since in the academic world as in the political and business worlds several generations of those who have plotted to destroy what they told the voters they were defending are now trying to cover their tracks.

What is so extraordinary about the quasi-religious fervour of Toynbee's talk of temples and divinity is the name of the conference he was addressing - of *"Institutions for the Scientific Study of International Relations"*. This description also displays an arrogance and assumption that their analyses (unlike those of others who may believe in national parliaments, democracies and sovereignty for instance) are uniquely "scientific". This is reminiscent of both Nazi and Communist views of political affairs. That human and international affairs are matters of judgment, uncertainty, cultural diversity, ethnic loyalties, geographic idiosyncrasy and religious convictions, and *not* conducive to mathematical assessment or purely objective methods, does not disturb the "scientist" who has "worked it all out" and "knows what is best" because he has "understood history".

This blind belief in the ability of scientists to sum up the world in a few trite phrases is seen in Toynbee's sentence:

> "Indeed the present economic unification of the world was implicit in the first navigation of the globe."

Like the present British Eurofanatics who claim that "Britain must be part of Europe because our trade is with Europe" (in fact only 43% of our trade is with Europe and that is loss-making) so Toynbee and his fellow would-be world governors equate economic trade with political unification. The whole purpose of trade is to increase wealth through the exchange of goods and services without needing to exchange whole populations. *Capital and goods move so that nations and cultures can maintain their cohesion and geographic locations and flourish without migratory disruption.* No nation would trade with another nation which had the same ideas, climate, produce, specialisation, manufactures and minerals. The whole purpose of trade is to exchange that which one needs for that of which one has a relative surplus. In exactly the same way the exchange of ideas cannot take place unless the variety of geographic, cultural, political, linguistic, and economic characteristics are embodied and identified in what have in the more advanced parts of the world, become *nations*. Just as economic trade needs diversity so world-wide intercourse needs national diversity. As the Germans have always admitted in their geopolitical theories, Western Europe is of little interest since they are competing with states of similarly advanced economic and social structures. Only in the East and overseas can German industry really prosper. (2) Their only interest in a giant superstate is political domination in Western Europe and the "clout" of a superstate to *control* their trading relations with less developed parts of the world.

Writing in 1931 Toynbee brings to bear on his fellow man all the procrustean force of the true collectivist and materialist (in either its fascist or communist form).

> "Mankind must either sacrifice its economic internationalism or bring its political and cultural life into conformity."

Even if this were a desirable objective the obvious past and continuing failure of these ideas disproves their feasibility. Even where there have been mass migrations - of say Hindus to Christian Britain or Muslims to Christian Germany - habits, dress, beliefs, family forms and places of worship have been recreated and have remained distinct. The former Yugoslavia is a far older case, thus proving that time strengthens rather than lessens such human diversity. A good example of language stability over many centuries is the return of ethnic Germans from various parts of Eastern Europe and the former Soviet Union, speaking a kind of German which died out long ago in the fatherland. In the USA Red Indian tribes prefer to maintain (where they can) the few tribal lands remaining to them, persuading new industries (even gambling licencees) to locate on their land for the benefit of their tribe and people. For centuries the Israeli nation had no homeland at all, but now they have realised their aim and even revived the Hebrew language (and no human nation was so internationalist as the Jews).

So free international trade would be impossible without nations just as the free exchange of ideas is impossible without free individuals. Human diversity which is not contained within geographically distinct nations recreates itself in far more risky environments elsewhere - where both host and minority communities feel under threat.

But Toynbee himself provides the most damning indictment of his own ideas. Writing just before Hitler came to power, and after the post-first-war League of Nations had been founded to "put an end to war" (!), he wrote:

> "More progress has been made towards overcoming the anarchy in political relations between states than had been made in the previous four centuries witness such successes as the League of Nations, the Treaty of Paris for the Renunciation of War as an instrument of national policy ..."

There followed of course 60 million deaths in the Second World War, millions more under the Stalin purges, Chinese communism, the Korean war, the Vietnam war, the Chinese invasion of Tibet, the Falklands War, the Gulf war, the Iran-Iraq war, the Russian invasions of Czechoslovakia and Hungary, the Bosnian war, the Afghanistan war and many more. For a fifty-year period this must rank as a grotesque failure for the institutions based on the ideas of Arnold Toynbee. Indeed today, according to the Institute for the Study of Conflict, there are 31 wars in various parts of the world, virtually all involving nations *seeking* sovereignty from oppressive supranational powers.

So nationhood (or "political anarchy" as he calls it) will be ended, writes Toynbee, echoing Warburg before the Senate Committee (see chapter 7) and anticipating Kohl's threats if the European Union should not materialise as he wished:

> "either by agreement or by force."

Toynbee's ideas also reflect fascist theory when he praises the 'western art of war' as a tool for spreading his world order:

> "One element of western culture however which oriental peoples could not afford to reject was the western art of war ... in adopting one element of western civilisation the oriental peoples were necessarily drawn into the adoption of others."

Toynbee is in no doubt about the importance of conferences of people like himself, and his ideas of power and influence include all those kinds of profession which became so prominent in the Bilderberg Group:

> "... our members include a large proportion of those persons by whom, in every country, public opinion is formed: the journalists, the businessmen, the professors, the bankers, the lawyers, and in their private capacities, the military and naval officers and civil servants."

Note the absence from this list of MPs, political parties, party activists, writers etc. Here we have the attitude of the corporatist in all its glory. All this has of course a purpose:

> "Here, ready for immediate use, we have a most effective means for informing the public in each of our countries in a scientific, objective, dispassionate way of what the public in other countries is feeling and thinking. Let us make use of these means to prepare public opinion for the next great conference."

These corporatists - the best example being the Bilderberg group - are not only unaccountable to national or international opinion but they actually consciously prevent reporting to a wider audience. They nevertheless expect their "scientific" solutions, arrived at by people like themselves, unquestioned in public forums and untried in democratic societies, to be picked up and implemented by the world in general.

In the absence of democratic challenge and the public exposure of such people, the Toynbees of this world rest secure in the knowledge that they can continue to pull the strings of nations and "democracies" in their construction of the new world order. A terrible prospect for free men and free nations.

(1) See especially chapter 10.

(2) Helmut Kohl's recent wooing of China, as Anglo-Saxon animosity towards Peking has increased, is of particular relevance as is Germany's massive investment in the former Soviet Union.

6

JOSEPH RETINGER: FROM PERSONAL INTRIGUE TO COLLECTIVE POWER

> "You and I were both subjects of good old Emperor Franz Joseph. Come let us now join forces and conspire together."
>
> Retinger to Alcide de Gasperi, Prime Minister of Italy.

As Disraeli noted, "the world is governed by very different personages from what is imagined by those who are not behind the scenes". Joseph Retinger was a Polish socialist who spent his life deliberately trying to organise and influence "behind the scenes" democratically elected politicians to support moves and plan strategies which their own electorates, had they ever been informed, would have rejected.

For those who regard investigations into the Bilderberg Group and other elite organisations as no more than the "wild excesses of conspiracy theorists" it is pertinent to note the motivations and methods of those who have founded such groups and how they influence what are generally regarded as "democratic" governments.

Retinger betrays in his remarks to de Gasperi his penchant for intrigue, his view of Europe as a new empire in the making and his use of Prime Ministers and royalty to achieve his ends rather than public discourse and the democratic process.

His biographer and friend John Pomian wrote of Retinger: (1)

> "Retinger's ideas were always stimulating and intriguing. It left room for the other person to invent his own definitions,

> to complete with his own suggestions, to add and to discard and finally to espouse the end product of it all as his own idea."

Pomian quotes ambassador Pietro Quaroni's view of Retinger:

> "A Pole once remarked to me many years ago: Every Pole has conspiracy in his blood. (with Retinger) first came very vague hints concerning desirable aims, then as I gradually caught on, a few details, and then, measuring them out knowingly, he revealed some further details then a few names ..."

Having flown to England at the beginning of the war Retinger hosted a series of lunches for European Prime Ministers who had fled their Nazi-occupied countries. He regarded London, where he was based for the rest of his life, not as a home but as a place from where he could better realise his aim of creating European "unity" - that most convenient word which can mean either an harmonious association or a unified whole. He always rejected the idea of taking a British passport and retained his stateless Europeanism "however inconvenient this was for his travels" as Pomian notes.

So Retinger, the most successful proponent of a European state, was a man without roots, without a country to which he would give allegiance, without a passport to define him and with no physical home other than a London flat.

After the war Retinger approached that institution which has always attracted the supranational, anti nation "elites" - the Royal Institute of International Affairs at Chatham House in London.

> "In 1946 I felt the time had again come to make a new effort in the direction of the unity of Europe. I made a start by giving a lecture at Chatham House."

Soon Retinger founded the "Independent League for Economic Cooperation", a typically innocuous sounding title, intended to lull the gullible into believing that only economic cooperation was the aim, not political federalism. The word "independent" seems at first sight comforting but when one recognises that "independence from national governments" meant ultimately a power over those governments, then Retinger's organisations take on a rather different stamp:

> "Neither van Zeeland nor I had to alter any of our views on Europe but we thought it better to limit ourselves to practical suggestions on economic matters."

Fortunately for the United Kingdom, the Labour government of 1945 to 1951 was only too aware of the nature of Retinger's elite and the then Chairman of the Labour Party National Executive Committee Manny Shinwell wrote to Churchill, then in his (later to be rejected) "European unity" mood:

> "It is felt that the subject of European Unity is much too important to be entrusted to unrepresentative interests and ... the number of private individuals selected by an unknown process robs the Congress of any representative character"

This we can contrast with the recent corporatist and anti-democratic remarks of the President of the British Chambers of Commerce:

> "Europe is far too important to be left to politicians."

It is important to note that Labour Party leaders like Shinwell and Bevin were opposed then to the views shared by Tory businessmen and European socialists. In other words, then as now, the issue was not so much left or right as democratic or corporatist, national parliaments versus supranational elites.

When the Labour Party proposed as a Vice President of the "European Assembly" the Government Chief Whip, he was rejected and a Conservative was elected instead. As Pomian remarks:

> "The Assembly knew that it would have to fight with governments and didn't want to elect leaders who would have a double allegiance."

This is precisely the point made in our book *Treason at Maastricht - the destruction of the Nation State* when we quoted the breach of allegiance committed by the two British European Commissioners, Brittan and Kinnock who, as Privy Counsellors in the UK had sworn allegiance only to the Queen. Allegiance, like sovereignty, is indivisible.

When Retinger, flush with CIA funds channelled through the "American Committee on a United Europe" approached the German "Prins zur Lippe Biesterfeld", otherwise known as Prince Bernhard of the Netherlands, in order to found the Bilderberg Group, he used the good offices of Paul Rykens, the then Chairman of Unilever. From the very beginning Bilderberg was not just a covert political group but a corporatist clique, comprising bankers, businessmen and press barons. It was very much in the Retinger tradition of pursuing his aims through elites of every order - business, banking, politics, journalism and royalty.

Unilever features continuously in the movement towards the destruction of nation states. As the purveyor of mass market foods and detergents Unilever, like many other global marketers of simple products, sees people not as culturally sensitive individuals with allegiance to a historical national tradition but simply as consumers to be stimulated by effective advertising to act in one country as in any other. Nations provide legal, constitutional, cultural and democratic barriers to this aim and must be swept aside in the search for corporate profit. Such corporatists therefore make common cause with their ostensible enemy - trade unions and socialists who have different reasons for pursuing the destruction of nations and the conservative traditions they represent.

The 1996 Bilderberg meeting in Toronto was attended by Morris Tabaksblat, the Chairman of Dutch Unilever. Floris Maljers, Chairman in 1993 attended Bilderberg that year. It was a former, senior executive of Unilever - pension paid by the company - who chaired a Conservative selection meeting in Yorkshire at which good candidates were rejected in favour of a lady who was already an MEP for a constituency 250 miles away and who will, should she be elected, represent simultaneously her Yorkshire constituents in Westminster and the people of Essex in the European parliament - at a combined cost to the taxpayers of £1.15m *per annum.*

A Unilever Vice Chairman again featured when a certain Niall Fitzgerald, Chairman of the CBI's "Europe" Committee recently poured scorn on the British people's right to self-government outside the European Union. Unilever certainly qualifies as the kind of dangerous unaccountable corporatists who intervene covertly to influence the direction of "democratic" politics.

So when Retinger started his Bilderberg Group he was following a life-long philosophy, summed up by his biographer:

> "Retinger always believed that public opinion follows the lead of influential individuals. He much preferred working with carefully selected individuals to publicity on a massive scale."

Like one of his mentors, Arnold Toynbee (notes Pomian), Retinger:

> "(believed) religions exert a paramount influence on the life of civilisations ... Hence from the beginning of the movement an attempt was made to enlist the support of the Churches. At the Hague (congress) the Papal Nuncio was present and subsequently Cardinal Cento."

The involvement of the Roman Catholic church in the various attempts to reconstruct a European state was evident in the Vatican having been the first country to recognise the Hitler regime and the prominence of Roman Catholics like Helmut Kohl in the "Christian Democratic Parties" of Europe. However the recent poor electoral results for such parties in Germany and Italy now demonstrate how little support these pan European ideas have among the electorate - not least when the Churches seem to have been involved in much of the corruption of the post war period within Christian Democrat parties.

Nowhere is the rejection of Helmut Kohl's eurofanatical aims more pronounced on the continent than in his own country. Needless to say the British people have not been made aware of this by, for instance, the BBC which has, as in the 1930s, pursued a somewhat different agenda. The European institutions of course have an incentive to prevent national electorates from knowing about opposition to eurofederalism in other countries, since otherwise accusations of "being isolated in Europe" might fall rather flat. Germany's "democracy" being as flawed as the French and the Italian, a too ready acceptance of authority by the German people and the politically oppressive nature of party systems based on proportional representation (see page 107) have hitherto insulated German political leadership from the views of the electorate. But times change and the recent book by Professor Gunter Rohrmoser *"Germany at the cross roads - turning back or going under"* shows the risks taken by the German Conservatives have been as catastrophic as the actions of the British Conservatives;

> "... 70% of Germans support a Europe of nations. If Helmut Kohl continues with his obsession with Europe, ignoring all other interests, he will lead the Christian Democrats to a Waterloo, from which they will never recover."

The reference to Waterloo is certainly a compliment to the anti EU attitudes of the British people - if not their government.

But to return to Retinger and the beginnings of his post war intrigues. He was undoubtedly successful beyond his wildest dreams, mainly because he utilised the same arguments not so successfully paraded by the Nazis - that a united Europe was a guarantee against Soviet Communism (an argument repeated many times by those on trial at Nuremberg). Thanks to the efforts of Retinger and others the foundation of the Council of

Europe became the embryo European Government. Pomian writes:

> "It was composed of Ministers, a parliamentary Consultative Assembly and an independent Secretariat - the prefiguration of a Government, parliament and Civil Service."

Retinger's work was bearing fruit and:

> "Nearly all the key figures in the Assembly were held by (European Movement) members."

It is one thing to create out of personal contacts and political intrigue an organisation and even a quasi government, but what good is a government without something to govern? How can a secretive organisation obtain the loyalty or even acknowledgment of its "subjects"? But as Pomian points out in his biography of Retinger, the only thing that matters is that a forum with a name and the "right kind of people" "behind the scenes" can take control of national governments. Here is how Pomian describes the process:

> "Inside Europe political opinion within a country can be influenced by the views and wishes of European nations. A good deal of pressure can be brought on a country which is out of step with its partners and this is almost always effective enough as none is sufficiently strong to disregard others for long. That is why the Common market, or any other European grouping can be made to work."

Out of personal contacts, therefore, comes collective coercion. This is how one or two individuals with an idea, the right personal connections and a fanatical and persistent belief in a new empire can create that empire. This is how a group of individuals invited to *cooperate* can be turned into a supranational *collective*, forced into a direction which the electorates of those individual nations would never have supported.

It is perhaps not surprising given this extraordinary victory for these corporatist cliques that they have a smug and arrogant opinion of themselves. Pomian writes:

"... today there are few key figures on both sides of the Atlantic who have not attended at least one of these meetings. What is perhaps more important is that everyone is flattered to receive an invitation."

Pomian quotes a Hungarian diplomat, Paul de Auer on Bilderberg:

"Mr de Auer wearily waved his hand and said: 'Monsieur, in politics those things are important which important people think are important.' By this simple rule the Bilderberg Group is certainly important."

Whether the activities of groups like Bilderberg are a "conspiracy" is a matter of personal vocabulary. But for those who plan behind the scenes, taking great care to conceal their activities, accusations of conspiracy have become their best defence. Much of this is due to an uninformed journalist profession and indeed the deliberate inclusion of some journalists and newspaper owners *within* the secretive group.

"How can it be a conspiracy if I, a journalist, know about it?" Indeed the excluded party is not the journalist but democratic electorates and the open process which is supposed to characterise democratic discussion. By those values Joseph Retinger's Bilderberg Group is certainly anti-democratic.

(1) This and other quotations in this chapter are from *Joseph Retinger, Memoirs of an Eminence Grise*, by John Pomian, University of Sussex Press 1972.

7

THE BILDERBERG GROUP

Between 1973, when Edward Heath's European Communities Act came into force and 1993, when the Maastricht Treaty legislation passed through the House of Commons, the United Kingdom, its democracy, the jurisdiction of its courts and the sovereignty of its parliament were largely destroyed.

Such an enterprise did not happen without deliberate intent, secrecy and the active collaboration of leading British politicians and businessmen. It could also not have happened unless it had been:

1. In the interests of a powerful force (certain political interests in the United States bent on creating a United States of Europe)
2. Based on a well thought out scheme (the historical German and French plans for a Eurostate)
3. Implemented by undemocratic means (powers which allowed the executive to bypass Parliament); and
4. Supported by a clique of British establishment figures who have claimed that, since the Empire became a Commonwealth, the United Kingdom was finished and its political and economic influence of no account. Echoing similar attitudes in 1914 and 1939 they so appeased the demands of our adversaries that they failed to protect either our national interest or even our constitution.

There is a secretive group which, in its foundation and in its core (if not in all those who have attended its meetings) has played a central role in this process - the Bilderberg Group, founded in 1954 by Prince Bernhard of the Netherlands.

Bernhard was a Nazi party member from 1933 until 1937,[1] who resigned one day after his controversial marriage to the future Queen of the Netherlands. The timing of his resignation letter (in order to marry into the Dutch royal family) tells us more than his later support for the Allied cause. An unsigned copy of Prince Bernhard's resignation letter was found in the National Archives, Washington. The letter ended "Heil Hitler" - hardly a renunciation of the Nazi party. In 1934 he was the subject of a report by a US Congress committee which identified him as an SS officer attached to the Nazi government's principal industrial ally, I G Farben.[2] He resigned from Bilderberg in 1976, the year in which he was revealed by the Dutch Government's Donner Commission as having accepted a US$1m bribe from the Lockheed Corporation.[3] As reported in the *Times* of 10th and the 12th June 1976, one of the witnesses, on his way to the Commission with tapes and documents, was run over by a car and his briefcase stolen. That witness was a British zoologist, Tom Ravensdale, former PR officer with the World Wildlife Fund of which Prince Bernhard was president.

The origins of this secretive international group of businessmen, principally corporatist and socialist politicians, journalists (who conveniently forget their devotion to open democratic discussion when invited by Bilderberg) and a few misguided continental royals, lie in post-Second-World-War American-European relations.

Bilderberg apparently represents and attracts the kind of people who regard corporatist and state power as more "efficient" than the wishes of individuals, families and nations. The former American ambassador to Bonn, George McGhee, is on record as saying that, **"The Treaty of Rome which brought the European Community into being was nurtured at Bilderberg meetings"**.

Richard Aldrich, a former CIA operative, wrote in Diplomacy and Statecraft, March 1997:

> "Although Bilderberg and the European Movement shared the same founders, members and objectives arguably

> Bilderberg constituted the more effective mechanism....it is clear that the Rome Treaty was nurtured at Bilderberg in the preceeding year."

Aldrich further asserts (and he should know) that the American Committee for a United Europe which shared so many "founders, members and objectives" with Bilderberg:

> "...reveals the style of early covert actions, not least the reliance on private organisations - albeit coordinated by a close circle of friends"

The minutes of the first Bilderberg meeting declared their aim:

> "... to evolve an international order which would look beyond the present day crisis. When the time is ripe our present concepts of world affairs should be extended to the whole world."

The key phrases, indeed code words for this self-appointed elite, include "international order" - a phrase common to both naive modern-day corporatists and the pernicious leaders of Nazi Germany. "When the time is ripe" indicates both the long-term planning of their project ("our present concepts") and an element of secrecy. The phrase "the whole world" reveals their supranational power cravings and the intention to eliminate untidy elements like national democracies.

Virtually all the leading Bilderberg figures are also members of the US-based Council on Foreign Relations which (despite the presence of many sound liberal and conservative inter-nationalists) was founded by the most fanatical of all "world government" proponents, Paul Warburg. Warburg's activities included being a director of IG Farben America which, during the Second World War, entered into technology transfer agreements with the Rockefellers' Standard Oil as well as benefiting from Standard Oil's monopoly in synthetic rubber which greatly enhanced Nazi Germany's foreign exchange earnings and its capacity to manufacture war materials. Iso-octane technology, essential for German aviation fuel was provided exclusively by Rockefeller's Standard Oil of New Jersey.[4]

It was Paul Warburg's son James who, in evidence to a US Senate committee in 1950, best articulated the aims of the world collectivists: "We shall have world government whether we like it or not. The only question is whether world government will be achieved by conquest or consent." So the principal European pillar of the Bilderberg group was a once well connected Nazi while the American pillar was a Rockefeller whose family company, Standard Oil, had been so helpful to the Nazi regime and had a joint venture from the 1920s to 1942 with the Nazis' principal industrial ally (IG Farben).

James Stewart Martin, the former chief of the Economic Warfare Section of the Department of Justice, noted in his 1950 book "All Honourable Men":

> "a picture began to emerge of an enemy that did not need the services of spies and saboteurs. By agreement between German and American producers of magnesium (need for aircraft) production in the United States before the war was limited to no more than 5,000 tons per year. In contrast, Germany in 1939 alone used 13,500 tons and during the next five years consumed magnesium at the rate of 33,000 tons per year."

Reuters reported (5.10.96) on recently declassified American Intelligence documents which confirmed an August 1944 meeting between the SS and representatives of 7 German companies including Krupp, Roehling, Messerschmidt and Volkswagen. At this meeting in Strasbourg plans were made to build up wealth, power and industrial capacity abroad, "so that a strong German empire can be created after the defeat". A US Treasury Department analysis of 1946 reported that the Germans had transferred $500m out of the country before the end of the war. The aim was to prepare "for a post war commercial campaign" in other words the very kind of political-industrial planning which this book describes as "corporatist". German companies were encouraged to make alliances with foreign companies and the SS referred to the kind of international patent sharing agreements which Krupp made with US companies - and of which the above mentioned IG Farben-Standard Oil agreement was a classic example.

What politicians forget today is that in the late 1940s and early 1950s, before the Soviet Communist invasion of Hungary and the construction of the Berlin Wall, Germany was pursuing the same nationalistic (i.e. aggressive national) aims as in the 1930s but using the "building of Europe" as the means to this end. The links between Nazi Germany's Europe and Hitler's "world order" and today's crisis in Europe and the "New World Order" lie in this post-war period. This should not be surprising since 134 of von Ribbentrop's Foreign Office civil servants served under Adenauer and the same man appointed by Hitler as secretary of his "Europe Committee" (Heinz Twetschler von Falkenstein) was chosen by Adenauer in 1949 for a similar job as Director of the "European Division" of the West German Foreign Office. Consider the common theme in these three quotations from 1931, 1950 and 1951. First Dr Duisberg of IG Farben in 1931:

> "Only an integrated trading block will enable Europe to gain innermost economic strength ... the longing for a thousand year Reich cries for a new approach. For such a purpose we can use the mirage of a pan Europe."[6]

(From 1934 onwards IG Farben became the principal industrial vehicle for Hitler's war preparations.) Notice here what modern German leaders suppress but which the Nazis did not disguise - that for many Germans "Europe" and "das Reich" are one and the same.

Secondly Konrad Adenauer himself (the German founder of the European Community and indeed of modern Germany) in 1950:

> "A federated Europe will be a third force ... Germany has again become a factor with which others will have to reckon ... If we Europeans colonise Africa we create at the same time a supplier of raw materials for Europe."[7]

Even for Adenauer therefore "Europe" was a grand imperial ambition rather than just a national interest.

And from 1951, Adenauer's Minister of Commerce, Dr Seebohm (anticipating the British Government's favourite phrase!):

> "Does free Europe want to join Germany? Germany is the heart of Europe and the limbs must adjust themselves to the heart not the heart to the limbs."[8]

So some of the more naive cold war policies of the USA and the activities of Bilderberg have brought about the aims of aggressive German nationalism but have done so in the name of a "new international order" - and, of course, corporatism. The same names (Ford and Rockefeller[9]) whose companies had US directors on the board of American IG Farben (which used its funds to finance Nazi propaganda[10] and three of whose German directors were found guilty at Nuremburg) also part-financed both the major "new world order", corporatist institutions established after the First World War (the Council on Foreign Relations and the London based Royal Institute of International Affairs). Henry Ford (personally on the board of American I.G.) wrote *The International Jew*, a favourite book of Hitler whose activities Ford financed in the 1920s. In 1938 Ford received Germany's highest medal for non-Germans - the Grand Cross of the German Eagle.[11]

The supranational/collectivist and anti-nation attitude of the Royal Institute of International Affairs in London is best demonstrated by Professor Arnold Toynbee (Director of Studies at that institute) at the Fourth Annual Conference for the Scientific Study of International Relations in 1931 when he presented his paper "Prophecy in the Twentieth Century":

> "If we are honest with ourselves we shall admit that we are engaged on a deliberate, sustained and concentrated effort to impose limitations upon the sovereignty and independence of the sovereign independent states which at present ... divide the political allegiance of mankind."

It is of course not so much "dividing" the allegiance that worries these "world government" elitists but the fact that they themselves cannot attract such allegiance. The duplicitous Toynbee continues:

> **"And all the time we are denying with our lips what we are doing with our hands, because to impugn the sovereign- ty or the local national states of the world is still a heresy for which statesman or a publicist can be ostracised and discredited."**

Observers of incompetent and treasonous foreign policies pursued by British governments will not be surprised to hear that Toynbee had important intelligence and research posts in the British Foreign Office in both world wars.

But it was following the Second World War that the Polish-born Dr Josef Retinger, who had long intrigued to establish a Eurostate, set up the European Movement and with American CIA funds, the "American Committee on a United Europe" - the latter funding the former. Retinger interested (the native-German) Prince Bernhard of the Netherlands in his schemes and it was Bernhard who set up the Bilderberg Group named after the Hotel in Oosterbeek in Holland where the first meeting was held on 29-31st May 1954.

The early post-war CIA recruited many idealistic young veterans of the Pacific and European struggles. They sought to counter communism with an anti-Soviet conglomerate of European states. Even as late as 1975, by which time many of these were in senior positions there was pressure from the CIA for a "United States of Europe". As Vice-Chairman of the "No Campaign" in the 1975 UK referendum on European Community membership, Sir Richard Body MP was approached by two CIA officials who were unhappy about the anti-British and pro-European Community propaganda which the London CIA office had been told to disseminate. The then head of station in London was a certain Cord Meyer Junior who in 1954 was responsible for the funding of the European Youth Campaign. The campaign (for "European Unity") was the most active part of the European Movement between 1951 and 1959, not least because thanks to Meyer and others the CIA funded it to the tune of £1.34m. Needless to say no leading British newspaper published Sir Richard Body's evidence but a piece did appear in *Time Out*.[12]

Can the Bilderberg Group be described as a "conspiracy"? The core "Europhiles" who comprise the steering committee seem to be bent on a strategy which they conceal from voters and for which they have no democratic mandate - these few may perhaps be described at the very least as anti-democratic. Some attendees are just natural corporatists and socialists eager to attack national democracies while others attend because they are impressed by finding themselves part of a conclave of the "famous". For the sake of appearances other guests are invited, who totally reject their "one world" or even "one Europe" philosophy (Enoch Powell, Norman Lamont and Margaret Thatcher for example have each attended only once). But in general they are a group of the kind of people who believe in collectivist policies within nation states, the "organisation" of capital and labour by superior brains (like their own) and who, failing to convince voters at home, gravitate to the supra-national collectivism of larger and therefore more distant and less democratically accountable power bases. No wonder Margaret Thatcher (whose downfall was reportedly discussed and anticipated with such prescience at the 1989 Bilderberg conference) recently said, "It is an honour to be criticised by the Bilderberg Group".

Bilderberg has always discussed and promoted its power politics and designs behind closed doors. It has invited journalists of repute who never report their activities, and it invites leading politicians not as individuals but because they enjoy or are likely soon to enjoy positions of power. Both Heath and Blair were invited **before** they became leaders of their parties.

Bilderberg contends that *individuals* are invited for *discussions*, not *men of power* to decide or follow *an agenda*. But their meetings are shrouded in secrecy and are policed often by the armed forces of the countries in which they meet. Special security measures are taken, official cars meet leading participants at airports, special telephone and other communication links are provided direct to government and corporate headquarters. Only participants are allowed in the hotels they take over, delegates arrive anonymously, no agenda for the meetings are published and no delegate lists or communiqués are issued.

David Rockefeller expressed his gratitude to the "free press" of the democratic nations for their silence when he addressed a secretive reunion of Bilderberg in Sand, Germany in June 1991. The following is a translation from the French journal "Minute" of June 19th 1991.

> "We are grateful to the *Washington Post*, the *New York Times*, *Time Magazine* and other great publications whose directors have attended our re-union and have respected their promises of discretion for almost four decades."

The definition of a "great publication" is evidently one which publishes nothing of great significance. It is certainly one which realises that the "freedom of the press" is not the freedom of the people and the right to know is a right of governments, not of the governed. Rockefeller continued:

> "It would not have been possible to develop our world project if we had been subjected to the full fire of publicity all these years. But the world is now more sophisticated and disposed to move towards a world government which will not know war but only peace and prosperity for all mankind."

Those who meet behind closed doors, plotting the end of nation states, defying democracy and emphasising the elite nature of their group and the inadequacy of everyone else - such people are of course outraged if the democratic will does not fall in with their schemes. They also believe that *their* skills are precisely those which are indispensable to a governing elite. The banker Rockefeller therefore naturally asserts:

"The supranational sovereignty of an intellectual elite and of world bankers is surely preferable to the self-determination which has been practised for centuries past."

It is of course just because they fear that the world will reject their ideas that the Bilderberg elite meet in secret, seeking to establish their fantastic "new world" before the people can wake up and prevent its realisation.

Those attending are often financed out of Bilderberg funds and some are asked by their governments to attend officially (confirmed by Dr David Owen and Tony Blair), thus disproving the Bilderberg claim that everyone attends as a "private individual". Some have rather hazy memories about who paid for what and fail to enter their paid-for trips in the parliamentary register of members interests. Kenneth Clarke, like most politicians attending these meetings, claims complete ignorance of the background of the founder of Bilderberg.[13] Many will wish to know why those who owe their positions to national electorates should attend (at the expense of taxpayers or a secret group) meetings of an organisation founded by a former Nazi party member and SS officer, to pursue a secret agenda with leading international businessmen which, as we have seen in the "European Union", can have serious consequences for their own unconsulted electorates. Every MP is elected openly on a manifesto, democratically debated, to sit in his national parliament to make decisions solely in the interests of his own national electorate. Attending secret meetings of groups with a covert agenda, most of whose members were never elected, in well guarded locations is not at all what their voters had in mind.

The book *Treason at Maastricht* lists those who attended the 1993 Bilderberg meeting in Greece. They included three Britons - Kenneth Clarke, Tony Blair and Sir Patrick Sheehy (the then Chairman of BAT) **who within a few weeks of each other in early 1995 all wrote articles in British newspapers in support of the abolition of the Pound and of the Bank of England as a central bank** - i.e. in favour of a European

Single Currency. In 1995 and 1996 a new British name started to appear on the Bilderberg list of guests - John Monks, the President of the Trade Union Congress. A leading trade unionist fits Bilderberg's corporatist politics. Like corporate executives, civil servants and politicians, trade unionists believe in "organising" capital, labour, prices, parliaments and ultimately, of course, nations. Monks is now also advocating the abolition of the Pound.

Others who have regularly attended Bilderberg meetings over many years are:

Denis Healey, member of Communist Party while at Oxford, Councillor, Royal Institute of International Affairs (the UK pillar of the Committee on Foreign Relations, founded by a true believer in "World Government"). He wrote "Labour and a World Society" (1985). Involved with Bilderberg since its foundation in the early 50s, echoed the principal Soviet strategy of the post-war period - in *Neutralism* (1955) and *A Neutral Belt in Europe* (1958). Received Grand Cross of Order of Merit from Germany in 1979. British Delegate to Consultative Assembly, Council of Europe 1952-54, Chairman IMF interim Committee 1977-79, Secretary of State for Defence 1964-70, Chancellor of the Exchequer 1974-79. His *Who's Who* entry does not mention Bilderberg.

Eric Roll, Chairman of the Warburg Group which is a founder member of the "Association for Monetary Union in Europe". He was born "Erich" and wrote at least one book under that name. Educated in Austria, he has honours from the Austrian Government and the Légion d'Honneur from François Mitterand for his services to "Europe". From 1939 to 1941 he was special Rockefeller Foundation Fellow in the USA. He was the principal civil servant responsible for the policy of abandonment of the Commonwealth in 1962 and the commitment to the European Common Market (serving as deputy to Heath who led the UK delegation negotiating Common Market entry). His *Who's Who* entry does not mention Bilderberg.

Lord Carrington, Bilderberg Chairman for Europe and Canada. British Foreign Secretary from 1979 to 1982, Secretary of State for Defence 1970 to 1974, First Lord of the Admiralty 1959 to 1963, former Chairman of GEC. Carrington's *Who's Who* entry does not mention Bilderberg.

Edward Heath, who signed away the 800-year-old British constitution in 1972 and was awarded the "Karlspreis von Aachen" or Charlemagne Prize (and £75,000) by the Germans. He recently asserted in Parliament that it was no business of the electorate how much money he earned from his Parliamentary activities. He also claims that the surrender of Britain's international fishing rights was a matter of no interest except to a few fishermen! Heath said when signing the Treaty of Rome in 1972 that Britain was not sacrificing any national sovereignty, but when asked on BBC's Question Time on 1st November 1990: "The Single Currency, a United States of Europe, was all that in your mind when you took Britain in?" Heath replied: "Of course, yes." In the list of MPs' interests three out of six directorships listed by Heath involved investment in Communist China - he therefore had a personal interest in dismissing as "insignificant" the 1989 pro-democracy demonstration in Tianenmen Square which ended with 200 dead. He also recently asserted on BBC television that "You cannot have democracy with 1.3 billion people" - which explains his desire to create a massive European Union! When asked in the course of a long correspondence whether he was a freemason he replied by return that he was not. When asked if he was a Bilderberger no reply was forthcoming. His entry in *Who's Who* does not mention Bilderberg.

Martin Taylor, former Chief Executive of Courtaulds Textiles, is now Chief Executive of Barclays Bank, one of the prime movers behind the "Association for Monetary Union in Europe". His entry in *Who's Who* does not mention Bilderberg.

There seems little doubt, given the provenance of the Bilderbergers, that they have been and are the major force behind the destruction of the nation state and the creation of the Eurostate. The prominent British figures in Bilderberg have an inordinate number of awards and honours from European countries not particularly known for their democratic records. That they have always taken care to hold their meetings in secret, attempting to conceal both their agenda and membership, seem to indicate the nature of the group and the importance they attach to their activities.

There is a pernicious myth promoted by, among others, the BBC that those who oppose something they call "Europe" are "right-wing", "extremists" or "Europhobes" while those who promote the integration of our once sovereign nation into the new Eurostate are "liberal" "left wing", "Europhile" or "one nation" Tories. (A distinguishing feature of the "one nation" Tory is his persistence in giving away the one nation.) In fact it is those on what the BBC calls "the left" (inter- ventionist Tories or Fabian Socialists) who have designed and plotted the destruction of our nation and have most in common with the aims of 1930s' fascism. As we have seen, the principal organisation promoting the "European Union" was founded by a former Nazi party member and SS intelligence officer and the model on which today's Europe is unequivocally built is Hitler's 1942 plan for a "European Economic Community":

Hitler's Europe	**Today's Europe**
"Europäische Wirtschafts gemeinschaft"	European Economic Community
Lebensraum (living space)	European Space
Collective "access" to basic commodities	Common energy, fishing and agricultural policies
European Currency System	European Exchange Rate Mechanism
Europabank (Berlin)	European Central Bank (Frankfurt)

European Regional Principle	Committee of the Regions
Common Labour Policy	Social Chapter
Economic and Trading Agreements	Single Market
European Industrial Economy	Common Industrial Policy
"The transformation of the laws of supply and demand"	Resistance to GATT
"Replacing capital with organised labour"	European Works Councils

Furthermore the methods used to bring about this destruction of European nations are identical to Hitler's use of "Notstands-gesetze" (emergency laws) to bypass the German parliament and people - so adroitly exploited by the British government when using Treaty law to bypass our own parliament. Adolf Hitler of course came to a sticky end - British ministers who adopted a similar device have featured prominently in the honours list.

Further details of the new Europe under German control were contained in a 1941 report prepared for Secretary of State von Weizsäcker by Albrecht Haushofer, Rudolf Hess adviser and son of the "Geopolitician" Karl Haushofer.

The principal theme of the proposals was a federal structure for continental Europe centred on the German Reich of 1914 with varying degrees of association for different countries. Poland and the Czech and Slovak lands would be Reich "protectorates" which would form a common economic system with the Reich. Then there would be a group of "confederate" or "dependent" countries - Latvia, Lithuania, Estonia, Slovenia, Croatia and Serbia, with which the Reich would have agreements on the movement of people. Then there would be a group of "allied" countries - Finland, Greece, White Russia and the Ukraine - which would enjoy defence and economic agreements with the Reich. Finally all these countries, plus Sweden, Norway, Denmark, Switzerland and Italy would form a European Union.

It is more than interesting to note that Holland, France and the United Kingdom were excluded altogether and that these were also the three countries which Sir Roy Denman, former European Commissioner, arch Hitler appeaser and promoter of Britain's role in a federal Europe, claimed in his recent book would have been "saved" had Britain not gone to war with Hitler in 1939.

The idea of various levels or "circles" of countries involved with Germany's Europe is of course well known today and Haushofer claimed he believed in a series of alliances between nation states rather than a European superstate. However the Nazis' idea of sovereignty was that the nations should be ruled by Germany's puppets or by kindred regimes as in Spain and Italy. Haushofer believed in the central imperial power of Germany, rejected the territorial outcome of the First World War, and regarded Austria as a "state without a national personality" which should therefore belong to Germany. With such beliefs Haushofer could hardly be any more relied upon to sustain free associations of nation states than the more aggressive Nazi theorists. It is nevertheless disturbing that even a well regarded Nazi foreign affairs expert in the 1940s was proposing a less rigid "Europe" with less apparent coercion than is evident in the plans of Helmut Kohl and Jacques Delors.

In summary, the Bilderberg Group consists of (Continental) royalty, politicians, bankers, Press barons, leaders of industry, officials from the Foreign Offices of many countries, always including senior representatives from the UK, USA, Germany, Netherlands, France and Italy. It seems to have been the principal organisation which promoted and has for forty years nurtured the idea of a federated European superstate as a prelude to some form of world government. This state is founded on the same eleven elements as Hitler's 1942 plan for Europe under Nazi domination. The core seems to consist of the kind of people who regard corporatist and state power as more efficient than the views of individuals, families and nations. They seek as allies, and apparently with some success, many of those elements (or their descendants) in the British political and media establishment who would have made peace with Hitler and thus accepted, even welcomed, his plans for a united Europe.

In all this Bilderberg is adroitly assisted by the Foreign Office who misused Crown Prerogative to bypass Parliament and sign the Maastricht Treaty, thus establishing the foundation of the Eurostate. They promote the pernicious myth that the EEC and its successor forms have "preserved the peace in Europe" when this was the achievement of NATO alone - a free alliance of *sovereign nations*. Nowhere is that fact better demonstrated than in Bosnia today where the EU and UN failed (Germany and Belgium being principal arms suppliers to the warring factions as French and British troops struggled on the ground) and NATO succeeded.

Once again our sovereign nation is imperilled by powerful corporatist forces which aim to establish a supranational state which by its very size will be beyond democratic control. Who are those who constitute and finance the Bilderberg Group? Are their origins in personalities and corporations which aided the Nazi cause, and are their covert methods consistent with the national democracies they claim to represent? Can ignorance and naivety excuse modern politicians' frequent attendance at secret meetings of unaccountable international groups? Do the activities of this secretive organisation not reveal the true nature of that which they have so long nurtured - the European Union?

(1) See Gerard Aalders and Coen Hilbrink "de affaire Sanders, Spionage en intriges in herrijzend Nederland", The Hague, 1996, pages 130-132, and Nazi Party archives, now at the National Archive, Washington DC, RG59, Department of State Decimal file Box 6435 Folder 856.00B/12-1047.

(2) US Congress House of Representatives. Special Committee on Un-American Activities, 73rd Congress, 2nd session No 73-DC-4 Government Printing Office 1934.
Plus evidence of Max Ilgner, Head of IG Farben espionage at his trial before the Nuremburg Military Tribunal.

(3) Dutch Donner Commission report 1976 and *The Times,* August 28th 1976. Only the Queen's threat to abdicate if her husband were put on trial prevented legal proceedings.

(4) Evidence of Dr Oskar Loehr IG Farben, US Senate Hearings before Subcommittee of the Committee on Military Affairs "Elimination of German Resources for War", July 2nd 1945. Government Printing Office 1945.
Plus frequent reports from US Embassy Berlin to the State Department during the 1930s.

(5) Exposed by the *Frankfurter Rundschau* September 1951 forcing Chancellor Adenauer to admit to Parliament that the accusations were true on October 16th 1951.

(6) In a book by the Nazis' chief "Geopolitician" General Karl Haushofer.

(7) Konrad Adenauer, *Rheinischer Merkur,* May 20th 1950.

(8) Dr Hans Christian Seebohm, Speech 15th September 1951.

(9) Moody's Manual of Investments 1930, p. 2149.

(10) US Congress House of Representatives, Special Committee on Un-American Activities. Investigation of Nazi Propaganda Activities, 73rd Congress, 2nd session hearings 73-DC-4 GPO 1934.

(11) *New York Times* August lst 1938 (plus picture) and US State Department, Decimal file, National Archive, Washington DC "Money Sources of Hitler", report from US Embassy in Berlin.

(12) "Uncle Sam goes to Market" *Time Out* May 23-29th 1975 and the author's conversations with Sir Richard Body MP.

(13) *The Times* Diary May 24th 1995 and later correspondence with Mrs Lynn Riley - in possession of the author.

(14) *Treason at Maastricht - the destruction of the Nation State* by Rodney Atkinson and Norris McWhirter, 2nd edition, Compuprint Publishing 1995

8

BILDERBERG MEETINGS: ATTENDEES 1995 AND 1996

ATTENDEES 1995:

Chairman

Peter Carrington - Chairman of the Board, Christie's International plc, Former Secretary General, NATO

Honorary Secretary General for Europe and Canada

Victor Halberstadt

Professor of Public Economics, Leiden University, Netherlands.

Honorary Secretary General for U.S.A.

Casimir A. Yost - Director, Institute for the Study of Diplomacy, School of Foreign Services, Georgetown University, Washington.

CH - Joseph Ackermann - President of the Executive Board, Credit Suisse

I - Giovanni Agnelli - Chairman, Fiat S.p.A.

I - Umberto Agnelli - Chairman, IFIL S.p.A.

FIN - Mariti Ahtasaari - President of the Republic of Finland

USA. - Paul A. Allaire - Chairman, Xerox Corporation.

P - Luis Mira Amaral - Minister of Industry and Energy, Portugal

USA - Dwayne O. Andreas - Chairman, Archer-Daniels-Midland Company, Inc.

P - Francisco Pinto Balsemao - Professor of Communication Science, New University, Lisbon; Chairman, Sojornal sarl; Former Prime Minister.

S - Percy Barnevik - President and CEO, ABB Asea Broan Boveri Ltd.

F - Claud Bebear - Chairman and CEO, AXA Group.

USA - Lloyd M. Bentsen - Partner, Verner Piipfert Bernhard McPherson and Hand, Former Secretary of the Treasury.

D - Christoph Bertram - Diplomatic Correspondent, Die Zeit; Former Director, International Institute for Strategic Studies.

TR - Selahattin Beyazit - Director of Companies.

ICE - Bjorn Bjarnason - Minister of Culture and Education

DK - Ritt Bjerregaard - Commissioner, European Communities.

CDN - Conrad M. Black - Chairman, The Telegraph plc.

Cem Boyner - Chairman, New Democracy Movement.

INT - Hans van den Broek - Commissioner, European Communities.

GB - E. John Browne - Chief Executive Officer, BP Exploration Company Ltd.

USA - John H. Bryan - Chairman and CEO, Sara Lee Corporation.

GR - Costa Carras - Director of Companies.

P - Maria Carrilho - Professor of Sociology.

E - Jamie Carvajal Urquijo - Chairman and General Manager, Iberfomento.

I - Adriana Cerretelli - Correspondent in Brussels, Il Sole/Sole Ore.

TR - Hikmet Cetin - Deputy Prime Minister; Former Minister for Foreign Affairs.

INT - Willy Claes - Secretary General of NATO.

USA - Jon S. Corzine - Chairman and Senior Partner, Goldman Sachs & Co.

CH - Flavio Cotti - Minister for Foreign Affairs.

GR - Theodore A. Couloumbis - President, Greek Foreign Policy Institute.

CDN - Devon G. Cross - Head of the Donner Canadian Foundation.

INT - Jose Cutileiro - Secretary General, Western European Union.

USA - Kenneth W. Dam - Mas Pam Professor of American and Foreign Law, University of Chicago Law School; Former Deputy Secretary of State.

B - Etienne Davignon - Executive Chairman, Societe Generale de Belgique; Former Vice Chairman of the Commission of the European Communities.

USA - Lynn E. Davis - Under Secretary for Arms Control and International Security Affairs, Department of State.

CH - Jean-Pascal Delamuraz - Vice-President of the Federal Council; Minister of Economy.

I - Marie-Josee Drouin - Executive Director, Hudson Institute of Canada.

DK - Uffe Ellemann-Jensen - Chairman, Liberal Party; Former Minister for Foreign Affairs.

USA - Thomas S. Foley - Partner, Akin, Gump, Strauss, Hauer & Feld; Former Speaker of the House of Representatives.

CH - Walter Frehner - Chairman of the Board of Directors, Swiss Bank Corporation.

USA - Thomas L. Friedman - Foreign Affairs Columnist, the New York Times.

CH - Fritz Gerber - Chairman and CEO, F. Hoffman-La Roche & Cop., A.G.

USA - David R. Gergen - Visiting Professor, the Terry Sanford Institute of Public Policy, Duke University; Senior Fellow, the Aspen Institute.

IRL - Dermot Gleeson - Attorney General of Ireland.

B - John J. Gloossens - President and CEO, Belgacom.

CDN - Allan E. Gotlieb - Former Ambassador to the United States of America.

GB - David Hannay - Permanent Representative, U.K. Mission to the United Nations.

FIN - Jukka Harmaia - President and CEO, Enso-Gutzeit Oy.

CH - Hans Heckmann - Vice Chairman of the Board of Directors, Union Bank of Switzerland.

N - Westye Hoegh - Chairman of the Board, Leif Hoegh & Co. AS; President, Norwegian Shipowners' Association.

USA - Richard C. Holbrooke - Assistant Secretary for European and Canadian Affairs, Department of State.

FIN - Philippe Jaffre - Chairman and CEO, Elf Aquitaine.

B - Daniel E. Janssen - Chairman of the Executive Committee, Solvay S.A.

USA - Peter Jennings - Anchor and Senior Editor, ABC News World News Tonight. (Canadian Citizen)

USA - Vernon E. Jordan Jr. - Senior Partner, Akin, Gump, Strauss, Hauer & Feld (Attorneys-at-Law).

USA - Peter R. Kann - Chairman and Chief Executive Officer, Dow Jones & Company, Inc., Publisher, the Wall Street Journal.

D - Hans-Peter Keitel - Chairman of the Board, Hochtief AG.

USA - Robert M. Kimmitt - Managing Director, Lehman Brothers Inc.; Former Under Secretary of State for Political Affairs.

USA - Henry A. Kissinger - Former Secretary of State; Chairman, Kissinger Associates, Inc.

CDN - Ralph P. Klein - Premier of Alberta.

GB - Andrew Knight - Non Executive Director, News Corporation.

INT - Max Kohnstamm - Former Secrary General, Action Committee for Europe; Former President, European University Institute.

D - Hilmar Kopper - Spokesman of the Board of Managing Directors, Deutsche Bank A.G.

NL - Pieter Korteweg - President and CEO, Robeco Group; Honorary Treasurer of Bilderberg Meetings.

A - Max Kothbauer - Deputy Chairman, Creditanstalt-Bankverein.

CH - Alex Krauer - Chairman and Managing Director, Ciba-Geigy Limited.

USA - William Kristol - Chairman, Project for the Republican Future.

D - Karl F. Lammers - Member of Parliament (Spokesman for Foreign Affairs, CDU/CSU).

GB - Norman Lamont - Member of Parliament; Former Chancellor of the Exchequer; Director of N. M. Rothschild.

F - Andre Levy-Lang - Chairman of the Board of Management, Banque Paribas.

E - Francisco Luzon Lopez - Chairman and CEO, Argentaria.

A - Alexander R. Maculan - Chairman, Maculan Holding AG.

TR - Serif Mardin - Chairman, Department of Islamic Studies, American University, Washington, D.C.

FIN - Bjorn Mattsson - President and CEO, Cultor Ltd.

CH - Helmut O. Maucher - Chairman of the Board and CEO, Nestle Ltd.

F - Thierry de Montbrial - Director, French Institute of International Relations; Professor of Economics, Ecole Polytechnique.

CDN - J. Fraser Mustard - President, Canadian Institute for Advanced Research.

NL - Her Majesty the Queen of the Netherlands.

PL - Andrzej Olechowski - Former Minister for Foreign Affairs.

GR - George A. Papendreou - Minister of Education.

USA - Arno A. Penzias - Vice President Research, AT&T Bell Laboratories.

D - Hans-Friedrich von Ploetz - State Secretary, Ministry for Foreign Affairs.

CDN - J. Robert Prichard - President, University of Toronto.

CH - David de Pury - Chairman, BBC Brown Boveri Ltd. and Co-chairman, ABB Asea Brown Boveri Group.

GB - Giles H. Radice - Member of Parliament; Chairman of the European Movement.

USA David Rockefeller - Chairman, Chase Manhattan Bank International Advisory Committee.

GB - Eric Roll - President, S.G. Warburg Group plc.

GB - Emma Rothschild - Director, Centre for History and Economics; Fellow, Kings College, Cambridge University.

INT/I Renato Ruggiero - Director General, World Trade Organization; Former Minister of Trade.

F - Francoise Sampermans - Chairman, Group Express.

ICE - Stephan E. Schmidheiny - Chairman, ANOVA Holdings Ltd.

D - Jurgen Schrempp - Chairman, Daimler-Benz AG.

CH - Wolfgang Schurer - Chairman, MS Management Service AG.

INT - Klaus Schwab - President, World Economic Forum.

DK - Toger Seidenfaden - Editor-in-Chief, *Politiken*.

USA - Jack Sheinkman - President, Amalgamated Clothing and Textile Workers Union, AFL-CIO.

USA - Nancy E. Soderberg - Deputy Assistant to the President for National Security Affairs.

GB - H. Dennis Stevenson - Chairman SRU Group and the Tate Gallery.

N - Thorvald Stoltenberg - Co-Chairman of the Steering Committee of the International Conference on the Former Yugoslavia.

IRL - Peter D. Sutherland - Former Director General, World Trade Organization; Former member, Commission of the European Communities.

S - His Majesty the King of Sweden.

GB - J. Martin Taylor - Chief Executive, Barclays Bank plc.

F - Jean-Claud Trichet - Governor, Banque de France.

E Federico Trillo Figueroa - Vice President and Member of Parliament (Partido Popular).

S - Ines J. Uusmann - Minister of Transportation and Communications.

D - Gunter Verheugen - Secretary General, Social Democratic Party.

FIN - Pertti Voutilainen - President, Merita Bank Ltd.

A - Franz Vranitzky - Federal Chancellor.

NL - Karel Vuursteen - Chairman of the Board, Heineken N.V.

GB - William A. Waldegrave - Secretary of State, Ministry of Agriculture, Fisheries and Food.

NL - Jacques Wallage - Parliamentary Leader PvdA (Labour Party).

USA - Stanley A. Weiss - Chairman, Business Executives for National Security, Inc.

USA - John C. Whitehead - Former Deputy Secretary of State.

INT/USA - James D. Wolfensohn, President of the World Bank, Former President and Chief Executive Officer, James D. Wolfensohn, Inc.

D - Otto Wolff von Amerongen - Chairman and CEO of Otto Wolff GmbH.

USA - Paul Wolfowitz - Former Under Secretary of Defense for Policy; Dean, Nitze School of Advanced International Studies.

KEY TO ABBREVIATIONS

A - Austria
ICE - Iceland
B - Belgium
INT - International
CDN - Canada
IRL - Ireland
CH - Switzerland
N - Norway
D - Germany
NL - Netherlands
DK - Denmark
P - Portugal
E - Spain
S - Sweden
F - France
FIN - Finland
GB - Great Britain
TR - Turkey
GR - Greece
USA - United States of America
I - Italy

Only 15% of those attending this meeting had ever been elected to a parliament. Only 4% had any connection with news media, half of them being *owners* rather than reporters.

LIST OF 1996 BILDERBERG ATTENDEES

THE UNITED STATES:

Paul Allaire [Chairman of Xerox]
Dwayne Andreas [Chairman, Archer-Daniels, Midland]
Lloyd Bentsen [former Treasury Secretary]
John Bryan [Chairman, Sarah Lee Corp.]
William Buckley [the NATIONAL REVIEW]
Jon Corzine [Chairman, Goldman Sachs]
Stanley Fischer [International Monetary Fund]
Charles Freeman [Former Assistant Secretary of Defence]
Richard Holbrooke [former Assistant Secretary of State]
Henry Kissinger [former U.S. Secretary of State]
Henry Kravis [Kohlberg, Kravis, Roberts]
Winston Lord [Assistant Secretary of State]
Sam Nunn [U.S. Senator]
William Perry [Secretary of Defence]
David Rockefeller [Chase Manhattan Bank]
Jack Scheinkman [Chairman, Amalgamated Bank]
George Soros [President, Soros Fund Management]
George Stephanopoulos [Senior Advisor to the President]
Alex Trotman [Chairman, Ford Motor Company]
John Whitehead [former Deputy Secretary of State]

CANADA:

Lloyd Axworthy [Minister of Foreign Affairs]
Conrad Black [Chairman, Hollinger Inc.,]
Jean Chretien [Prime Minister of Canada]
Frederik Eaton [Chairman, Eatons]
Al Flood [Chairman, CIBC]
Allan Gottlieb [former Amassador to U.S.]
Anthony Griffin [Hon. Chairman, Guardian Group]
Mike Harris [Premier of Ontario]

Paul Martin [Finance Minister]

Sylvia Ostry [Centre for International Studies, Univ. of Toronto]

Ted Rogers [President, Rogers Communications]

Red Wison [Chairman, Bell Canada Enterprises]

EASTERN EUROPE:

Andrzej Olechowski [Former Polish Foreign Affairs Minister]

Flavio Cotti [Foreign Affairs Minister, Czech Republic]

Cornelio Sommaruga [President, Red Cross Committee, Czech Republic]

Gyorgy Suranyi [President, National Bank of Hungary]

WESTERN EUROPE AND TURKEY:

Lord Carrington [Conference chairman: former NATO Secretary-General]

Martti Ahtissaari [Finnish President]

Giovanni Agnelli [Hon. Chairman, Fiat, Italy]

Anders Aslund [Carnegie Endowment for International Peace, Sweden]

Francisco Pinto Balscmao [Former Prime Minister of Portugal]

Percy Barnevik [President, ABB Asca Brown Boveri, Sweden]

Queen Beatrix [the Netherlands]

Franco Bernabe [CEO, Ente Nazionale Idrocarburi, Italy]

Carl Bildt [the UN High representative in Bosnia]

Frits Bolkestein [Liberal Party leader, Netherlands]

Jaime Carvarja Urquito [Chairman, Iberfomento, Spain]

Bertrand Collomb [Chairman, Lafarge, France]

George David [Chairman, Hellenic Bottling, Greece]

Etienne Davignon [Executive Chairman, Societie Generale de Belgique, Belgium]

Gazi Ercel [Central Bank of Turkey]

Emre Gonesay [Governor, Central Bank of Turkey]

Westye Hoegh [Chairman, Leif Hoegh & Co., Norway]

Jan Huyghebaert [Chairman, Almanij-Kredietbank Group, Belgium]

Jaakko Iloniemi [Former Finnish ambassor to U.S.]
Peter Job [Chief Executive, Reuters, Britain]
Lionel Jospin [Socialist Party leader, France]
Dietrich Karner [Chairman, Erste Allgemeine-Generali Aktiengesclischaft, Austria]
Andrew Knight [News Corp., Britain]
Max Kohnstamm [European Policy Centre, Belgium]
Phillipe Maystadt [Finance Minister, Belgium]
Ad P.W. Melkert [Social Affairs Minister, Netherlands]
John Monks [Union Leader, Britain]
Mario Monti [European Commissioner]
Theodoros Pangalos [Foreign Affairs Minister, Greece]
Jan Petersen [Conservative Party leader, Norway]
Malcolm Rifkind [Foreign Secretary, Britain]
Simon Robertson [Chairman, Kleinwort Benson Group, Britain]
Renato Ruggiero [Director-General, World Trade Organization]
Mona Sahlin [Member of Swedish Parliament]
Jurgen Schrempp [Chairman, Daimler-Benz, Germany]
Klaus Schwab [President, World Economic Forum]
Queen Sofia [Spain]
Peter Sutherland [former Director-General, GATT and WTO]
Morris Tabaksblat [Chairman, Unilever, Netherlands]
J. Martin Taylor [Chief Executive, Barclays Bank, Britain]
Franz Vranitzky [Chancellor of Austria]
Antonio Vitorino [Deputy Prime Minister, Portugal]
Karel Vuursteen [Chairman, Heineken, Netherlands]
James Wolfensohn [President, World Bank]

Of the 80 Bilderbergers attending the 1996 meeting 20% had been elected to a parliament and 6% were connected to news media, although none of the latter were real reporters.

9

THE NEW "DEMOCRATIC" FASCISM

When a European Community civil servant, Jacques Delors, threatened that he "would precipitate a crisis" if he did not get his way and when he boasted at a TUC conference in Britain that "Soon 80% of government decisions will be taken in Brussels", he spoke with the true voice of the fascist. Delors, like the framers and enforcers of the rule of the European Community, believes that the state and the bureaucrat are more important to an "ordered" society than nations and parliaments.

Delors' background in the Vichyite equivalent of the Hitler youth - the *Compagnons de France* - and his praise of one of Vichy's leading economists (whose watchword was "to govern is to plan") made him an ideal candidate (with the Vichyite collaborator François Mitterand) to force modern Europe into the shoes of 1940's socio-economic fascism.

The socio-economic fascist sees little role for political or democratic systems since he believes - sincerely - that the people's happiness can be guaranteed by a strong state and strong and disciplined corporations of capital and labour, suitably organised by himself! The American journalist Dorothy Thompson spent much time in Germany in 1940 talking to Nazi theorists about their plans for Europe. In the *Herald Tribune* of 31st May 1940 she wrote:

> "The Germans count upon political power following economic power. Territorial changes do not concern them because there will be no "France" or "England" except as language groups, little immediate concern is felt regarding

> political organisations ... No nation will have control of its own financial or economic system or its customs."

Helmut Kohl, like his German predecessors, has always believed that "political power would follow economic power". It was always easy to pretend (as all collectivists do) that trade needed to be "organised", administrators needed to be appointed, supranational laws needed to be passed and imposed merely to raise the level of wealth and mutual "cooperation". But after all that (unnecessary) structure was in place the true intent could be revealed, as Kohl has now done:

> "We want the political unification of Europe. Without monetary union there can be no political union and *vice versa*."

> "The construction of the house of Europe remains the only real guarantee of freedom and peace in the 21st century."

Reminiscent of Nazi national romanticism Kohl proclaimed:

> "The future will belong to the Germans ... when we build the house of Europe."

Kohl's statist and corporatist (and therefore anti-democratic) credentials have more recently been on display when he said that

> "The United Kingdom will join a single currency [i.e. the abolition of the Pound] because the City wants it."

Here is a genuine fascist idea - that the will of corporatists and financial institutions are bound to override the will of a democratic electorate. Kohl has become used to just such a system in Germany where even those who are elected to parliament are strictly controlled by the party hierarchy through proportional representation and the list system. (Those MPs on the party list are appointed solely by the party machine and never have to answer to voters directly. Half of all seats in the German Parliament are reserved for 'list' MPs.)

Kohl and Mitterand's France extended their control to the European Commission and the European Court. The Court admits it has a political agenda, not a legal one, and defended preventing publication of European Union documents by saying:

> "... although heads of government have repeatedly called for more openness their declarations were of an eminently political nature and therefore not binding on community institutions."

Recently an internal European Commission memorandum revealed the (successful) attempt by officials to suppress evidence of BSE in non-British beef in order not to upset the agriculture market (*The Times* 2nd July 1996).

The European Commission demonstrated its vicious corporatism in the treatment of Bernard Connolly, the "European" civil servant who was director of the department responsible for European Monetary Union. He was sacked for publishing a book critical of EMU and the political intrigues behind it. As Connolly described his persecution by the Commission:

> "They did not concern themselves with the arguments but attacked me personally. I was eccentric, a difficult character, an extremist and I had always been a little mad."

How typical of the weak and inadequate corporatists whose policies always cause chaos which they then blame on those who predicted or revealed that chaos. It is also typical that in the face of their own inadequacy such an organisation should regard lies and distortion as a legitimate tool of government. For it was the European Commission which delayed publishing its own survey showing a collapse in European business confidence and had to apologise for distorting the presentation of a poll to make European public opinion appear more enthusiastic for monetary union than was in fact the case.

Those who stoop so low do not flinch from the fascist persecution of individuals who defy them. Bernard Connolly, following his dismissal, had his pension rights questioned, his telephone was tapped and his wife was pressured and followed - brave new Europe!

In *Le Figaro* in May 1994 Claude Cheyson, the former French Foreign Secretary and European Commissioner, was interviewed. He admitted he could never have "constructed Europe" except in the absence of democracy. He claimed that the problems now facing France were due to the democratic debate during the French Maastricht referendum!

Another leading French politician, Raymond Barre, former Prime Minister, gave vent to his feelings about democracy:

> "I never have understood why public opinion about European ideas should be taken into account."

With such a background it comes as no surprise that a so-called "European Parliament", in elections to which hardly more than 35% of the people vote (25% in the UK), is a refuge for a small criminal community. The former French minister Bernard Tapie was sentenced to prison and his immunity as a French MP lifted. However he retains his immunity due to his position as a Member of the European Parliament and an application to lift that immunity was rejected by the "democrats" in that "parliament". In fact up to 1992 only 13 out of 66 requests to lift Euro MPs' immunity proved successful. Perhaps we should not be surprised that a European Union which loses about £6 billion in fraud every year and whose agricultural system is infiltrated by the mafia, should also be a haven for criminals.

A British MEP, Tom Spencer, struggling to put the European Union in a democratic light, wrote that the British should not complain since although European laws were forced on the British parliament they had been approved by the Council of Ministers (in which the British ministers are regularly outvoted), by the European Parliament (the same process) and approved by British civil servants (in non-public meetings). The new Eurofascist thinks that party manifestos, British general elections, accountable British MPs and Westminster parliamentary sovereignty have nothing to do with democracy and he therefore does not question their absence from the new law-making process in "Europe".

In these arrogant dismissals of our democratic heritage the Eurostate is well supported by the Confederation of British Industry and other corporatist organisations into which our less able executives are parked. The President of the British Chambers of Commerce was quoted in the *Times*:

> "Europe is too important a subject to be left to politicians alone."

But of course, we need the brilliant minds of the CBI and Chambers of Commerce, who were such vociferous supporters of the ERM - until it collapsed about their ears. How reminiscent of the CBI's forerunner, the Federation of British Industry, which as late as March 1939, at Dusseldorf, agreed a plan of economic cooperation with the "Reichsgruppe Industrie", a group of leading German industrialists whose Chairman was Gustav Krupp. Whether preparing for the abolition of the pound or setting the stage for the Second World War, the CBI (FBI) were guilty of either bovine stupidity or rank treachery. In any case the historical record of this organisation must be born in mind when, as they frequently do, the BBC interviews their representatives on what is best for "UK plc" as they are wont to call our country.

Politicians who have been responsible for the destruction of the British constitution also take a rather odd view of democratic procedure. When John Major resigned as party leader and was challenged by John Redwood one Major Cabinet colleague remarked of the secret ballot:

> "Don't tell me about a secret ballot. We'll find the toe-rags out."

Just the kind of democratic public servant whom we would wish to grace the Mother of Parliaments. No wonder that such attitudes are prominent among the Eurofanatic supporters of John Major.

One of the ways in which the fascist state controls the people is by maintaining the structures of democracy but emasculating them by buying the allegiance of public servants. When ministers in the Commons and Lords defend the institutions and policies of the European Union it is not clear to the public how those very ministers profit from those policies. Recently the *Sunday Times* investigated the leading Conservative spokesmen on agriculture - an area which is almost completely controlled by Brussels. It transpired that the leading spokesmen in the Lords and Commons had substantial agricultural interests and had each received between £50,000 and £150,000 in European grants, subsidies and the infamous "set aside" (payment for not growing crops). One thing is clear about Conservative government spokesmen on European matters - they represent their own financial interests, not the democratic interests of the United Kingdom.

Yet another method of tyranny practised by the lackeys and placemen of the Euro-state within the United Kingdom is the simple refusal to reply to criticism or even to parliamentary questions. The following exchange took place in the House of Lords in July 1995:

Lord Stoddart of Swindon (Labour) asked whether Her Majesty's Government will commission a cost/benefit analysis of the United Kingdom's membership of the European Union as distinct from United Kingdom access to the European single market.

Lord Henley: My Lords, the Government have no intention of carrying out such an analysis ... The Government consider the benefits of membership of the European Union to be self evident. (For a true assessment of the economic "benefits" of membership see chapter 10.)

The arrogance of power assumes much is "self evident" and any suggestion that there might be a competing power (the truth!) cannot be tolerated and so no honest enquiry which might question the "knowledge" of the State is allowed.

Three attributes characterise the fascist - faith in the power and right of the state, the suppression of dissidence and personal abuse as a weapon against the vulnerable (and a substitute for rational argument). All three were well demonstrated by that most eurofanatical Conservative MP (and Foreign Office Minister), Tristan Garel-Jones when he explained his vicious attack on a fellow Conservative MP:

> "I wanted to see your body floating down the river as an example to enemies of the State."

These violent words were well reflected in the verbal and even physical intimidation of Conservative MPs by Government Whips.

In the book *Treason at Maastricht*, in which Norris McWhirter and I analysed the destruction of the 800-year-old British constitution, I pointed out that, like the American Union (from which the Confederate states tried to escape), the European Union agreement signed at Maastricht and the Treaty of Rome which it amended also made no allowance or mechanism for withdrawal from the Union. A Dutch spokesman for the EU, Nikolaus van der Pas, recently heralded a future "civil war" in Europe:

> "There is no exit door ... It is all so [sic] vast and complicated to be compared to a sweet shop where you can just walk in and out."

Once again we see the imperialist necessity of Continental corporatism and collectivism. Freedom and responsibility, nationhood, democratic sovereignty - all are out of the question. This inward-looking, aggressive paranoia of the European Union is wonderfully summed up in the words of the French newspaper *Le Figaro* when recommending protectionist measures to cure the unemployment caused by "European" economic and social policies.

> "In order to save jobs in Europe it is the world that has to be changed."

How reminiscent of the rantings and ravings of Hitler and his henchmen. But of course the kind of fascist ideas and behaviour chronicled in this chapter are a natural consequence of the social, economic and constitutional structures established by the "European" Union, based on the Nazi plans of 1942. Those who forget history are condemned to relive it.

10

APPEASEMENT: OMINOUS PARALLELS

Although all political movements are based on a set of ideas which can be put down on one piece of paper, their realisation depends, ultimately, not on the thousands of activists convinced by those ideas but on the willingness of millions of people to "go along with" that political movement. For this to happen those behind the ideas and leading that political movement must identify *the kind of people who* instinctively follow that kind of political philosophy. They must convince *the kind of people who* will be attracted to certain key words or phrases, like "state", "compassion", "supranational" or "solidarity". What actually happens in the name of these flexible expressions is of course an entirely different matter.

The characteristics which determine susceptibility to a particular set of ideas are usually not social class or even wealth. Rather, basic attitudes are determined by family background and the kind of work traditionally pursued by members of a family or group of families. Family businesses are succesfully passed on from generation to generation on this basis just as certain families pursue political careers (Churchills, Hoggs, Hurds), journalism (Jays), acting (Redgraves, Mills) or socialism (Benns, Wilsons).

At the collective level of ideas the kind of people and parties (and wings of parties) who were most prominent in appeasement of the Nazis in the 1930s have been equally prominent in the secretive destruction of the British Constitution since 1972.

There is a particular mixture of political and economic beliefs which characterise those who were prepared to see a Europe united under German control in the 1930s - or at least were unwilling to resist it - and who are prepared in the 1990s to see their country become a province of a new "European" sovereignty. They believe in the wisdom and efficiency of political action, the power of the state, collective solutions to social and economic problems, supranational organisations, majority voting as the source of social wisdom and the irrelevance of nations and national parliaments. They combine socialist statism with corporatist capitalism, seeking to exploit the economic power of the latter to promote the political power of the former. They promote social and industrial "solidarity" by combining trade unionists, politicians and corporatist businessmen into "tripartite" collectives, ignoring the interests and suppressing the influence of individual voters and consumers.

This attitude towards social and economic management has been prominent in all Labour governments and in the post war Conservative governments of MacMillan, Heath and, to a smaller extent, Major. Even after the Second World War when it was evident that Soviet Communism was as significant a threat to Europe and the United Kingdom as the Nazi tyranny had been, a large element of the British Labour Party was bent on appeasement.

In his speech at Fulton in the USA in March 1946 (before the overthrow of the democratic Czechoslovakian regime and the murder of Jan Masaryk) Churchill described the threat from the Soviet Union's international socialism:

> "From Stettin on the Baltic to Trieste on the Adriatic an Iron Curtain has descended across the Continent. Police governments are prevailing in nearly every case and so far, except in Czechoslovakia, there is no democracy."

In response 105 Labour MPs signed a Commons motion calling on the Government to disassociate itself from Churchill's speech. This appeasement of post-war Soviet power came as naturally to many Labour MPs as appeasement of pre-war Nazi power. Labour voted throughout the 1930s against rearmament. In 1935, speaking against the Conservatives' re-armament proposals Attlee said;

> "There is no security in armaments and we shall be no party to piling them up".

Ramsay Macdonald the former Labour Prime Minister was particularly helpful to the Nazis. As Gilbert and Gott in their book The Appeasers write: (1)

> "Macdonald showed little hostility towards the new Germany. He was unwilling to protest against Germany's illegal rearming."

Macdonald told the German ambassador, Hoesch, that: (2)

> "From the very start he had not believed the reports of excesses and moreover he understood very well the character of and circumstances attending a revolution. He also understood the movement of young Germany and did not criticize it."

According to Hoesch's diary, Macdonald: (3)

> "...had a plan for detente. It was a plan which the British Cabinet knew nothing about. Hitler should visit England. He would receive a most friendly reception from the people and government."

Gilbert and Gott note:

> "Von Neurath, the German Foreign minister, noted in the margin of Macdonald's suggestion: 'absurd'."(4)

Another socialist of the period, Lord Allen of Hurtwood, imprisoned for refusing military service in the first war, was a supporter of the League of Nations and managed to appease both Stalin and Hitler with equal enthusiasm. In 1935 he met Hitler and Goering in Berlin and sympathised with German objections to the Treaty of Versailles. He told an audience in Oxford that Britain should "let Hitler have whatever he wants in Eastern Europe" and that "Germany should not only be given the colonies that had been hers before 1918 but also others". (5)

Lord Allen also attended a meeting in London in 1935 to launch the English language edition of a Soviet book on the construction of the White Sea-Baltic canal which Solzhenitsyn refers to as "a disgraceful book - the first in Russian literature to glorify slave labour". 250,000 men died on the canal in 18 months. While disguising the millions killed by Stalin, this socialist was pleased to help another mass murderer who described himself as a socialist.

The British left was well represented in the ranks of appeasers, the future Chancellor of the Exchequer Stafford Cripps wrote in the Socialist Weekly "Forward":

> "Every possible effort should be made to stop recruiting for the armed forces."

I devote a whole chapter to the beliefs of the socialist historian Arnold Toynbee in this book but here it is relevant to quote some of the pronouncements which made him very much a revered member of the group of appeasers in the Cliveden set. Like many of his ilk, Toynbee visited Hitler in 1936 - long after there were any doubts about the nature of the Nazi regime. Toynbee was "convinced of Hitler's sincerity in desiring peace and close friendship with England". He joined Lothian and other appeasers in sending a telegram to Baldwin, not long after Hitler's march into the Rhineland, welcoming the latter's declaration of a "plan for 25 years of peace" (!).

After the British government had made it clear they were "not considering the handing over of any territories held under British mandate" (to Germany) Toynbee, speaking in Hamburg said of the colonies:

> "We British are not so foolish as to think things must remain as they are. Obviously the very essence of human affairs is change and if it is not peaceful it will be violent change."

The usual configuration of appeasers, collectivists and admirers of state and supranational powers includes socialists, corporatist Conservatives and those who for some strange reason have joined something called the "Liberal" Party. Two excellent examples of the dangerous beliefs of British "Liberals" are Lord Lothian (in MacDonald's cabinet) and the former Prime Minister Lloyd George.

Lord Lothian became a Christian Scientist and in his Burge Memorial Lecture in 1935 advocated a universal federation of mankind. Up until 1938, when he eventually admitted his naivety, Lord Lothian believed that: (6)

> "the root of the present difficulty is that the Germans have got a case but nobody is really willing to make the concessions necessary to meet their claims."

He told Eden in 1936 that Britain should not deny to Germany a position of power: (7)

> "to which she is entitled by her history, her civilisation and her power... (she must be allowed to) escape from encirclement to a position of balance".

In 1939 after illegal German re-armament, hundreds of thousands of political prisoners, violent anti-semitism, religious persecution, the 1938 "Kristallnacht" and the military takeover of the Rhineland, Lothian could write: (8)

> "...many people, I think, felt that the internal persecution in Germany was in great part the result of the denial to Germany of the rights which other sovereign nations claim."

In 1935 Lord Lothian had told Hitler that he did not rule out a change in the political status of Austria and in 1937 he told Hitler that Britain "had no primary interests in Eastern Europe" (reminiscent of John Major's statement that the United Kingdom had "no selfish economic interest in Northern Ireland"). Needless to say Hitler was willing to take up Lothian on his offers.

With such a pedigree in the appeasement of the Reich's ambitions it is not surprising that Lord Lothian should appear on the list of British political figures most helpful to the German cause, drawn up by Albrecht Haushofer and submitted to Rudolf Hess before the latter's flight to Scotland in May 1941. (9)

That other great Liberal, Lloyd George found Hitler: (10)

> "the greatest living German... I only wish we had a man of his supreme quality at the head of affairs in our own country today."

And to the Sunday Times Lloyd George described Hitler as

> "...a man of great understanding and of a fascinating gift of conversation whose honesty deeply impressed me"

- to The Sunday Express he praised Hitler as:

> "a born leader of men, a magnetic, dynamic personality"

It is perhaps not surprising that today the leader of the Liberal Democratic Party, Paddy Ashdown reflects the same dangerous notions expressed by appeasers and Nazis alike:

> "I do not believe that the nation state is anything other than a recent historical invention. I do not believe it will always remain." (Hansard 18th December 1991)

> "Europe cannot stand still (at)...the level of integration at which we have now arrived. If Europe does not go forward it will start to go back" (Hansard 20th May 1992)

But as Gilbert and Gott point out: (11)

> "Appeasers were to be found everywhere, without distinction of sex, party or club."

And those best positioned to realise in practical policy the true dangers of their appeasement were of course Conservative Ministers. The most striking parallel with that period is in the positions of Chamberlain and Major and their respective principal advisers on foreign policy, Sir Horace Wilson and Douglas Hurd. Of Wilson, whose room at Number 10 gave him unrivalled power over Chamberlain's foreign policy even though he was not Foreign Secretary, an observer wrote; (12)

> "In all the critical years when swift bold strong action alone could have served our need, Wilson's temporising, formula-evolving mind reinforced and emphasised the weakness of the Prime Minister."

Just as one of John Major's colleagues remarked how the Prime Minister felt lonely on his own at night in 10 Downing Street, Lord Woolton wrote: (13)

> "I remember Wilson, after dining with me one night, leaving me early and saying I must go and look after my master: he's feeling very lonely just now."

Lloyd George remarked - reflecting the view of many - that Neville Chamberlain "did not rise above a provincial manufacturer of bedsteads" and his own father found him completely unsuitable for a political career. By way of comparison John Major himself admitted that he thought he could not rise to the top in any profession and therefore decided he could make a contribution to politics. One cannot help seeing direct parallels between the treatment of Chamberlain by Hitler and the superficially friendly but substantively dismissive approach of "my friend Helmut" to John Major. Indeed a similarly dismissive approach to John Major seemed to be taken by his own Chancellor of the Exchequer, Kenneth Clarke who blundered along on his own agenda, oblivious of government policy and party sensibilities. A similar role was played in the 30s by Sir Horace Wilson, ostensibly attached to the Treasury but in fact pulling the foreign policy strings in Number 10.

It was Horace Wilson who called in Lord Woolton, who as the chief of Lewis's, a Midlands department store, had closed its operations in Germany in protest at the behaviour of the Hitler regime. Sir Horace Wilson told Woolton that: (14)

> "Chamberlain strongly disagreed with his action and that he had no right to interfere in this manner in the foreign policy of the country."

But the most extraordinary and treasonous conduct of all leading Conservatives in this period was the activity of Sir

Samuel Hoare, the former cabinet minister, whom Churchill had sent to be ambassador in Madrid, a peripheral role which Hoare resented. In Spain, without the knowledge of the Foreign Office, he took up contact with Rudolf Hess and Albrecht Haushofer who were preparing (certainly with Hitler's approval) Hess's flight to Scotland and plan to make peace with Britain, as a prelude to the invasion of Russia. Despite a certain distaste for the crudities of National Socialism, Haushofer shared all the foreign policy aims of the Nazis while Hess was a loyal servant of the "Fuhrer". The Hess peace plan included a demand for the resignation of Churchill - a contingency which Sir Samuel Hoare greatly desired. Indeed he told his Nazi contacts that he "reckoned sooner or later with Churchill's resignation and that he (Hoare) would then be asked to form a government". (15)

Hoare told Prince Hohenlohe that he would only accept the post of Prime Minister if he could have a free hand in ending the war. Although there was much talk of Churchill's resignation there was no insistence on Hitler's. Hoare had already decided on a Foreign Secretary, R. A. Butler - who later became a typical Macmillan protege and early "Heathite" in post war Conservative governments.

The Germans saw frequent reports from Madrid that Hoare repeatedly sought contact with German nationals. Undoubtedly Hoare's treasonous conduct in time of war had led Hess to believe that his arrival in England would lead to a change of government. Indeed his *sine qua non* for negotiations was the resignation of Churchill, the feasibility of which Hoare's contacts with German officials had described.

Just as Hohenlohe had emphasised to Hoare Germany's need for Russian land and oil, so Hess made it clear to his British interrogators that Britain could keep its empire so long as Germany enjoyed free reign in continental Europe. That a British ambassador and former Home Secretary could have peddled this treason to the Nazi regime is extraordinary enough. Far more iniquitous was Hoare's elevation at the end of the war to "Viscount Templewood".

Another stab in the back for those who would not swallow the appeasement line was the dismissal of a certain Captain Aue from his post as Vice Consul in Hanover. He was a businessman, not a diplomat and was prepared to speak out against what he knew to be true about German rearmament. Complaints from the Hitler regime, anxious to keep their operations secret, were accepted without protest by the British government. A direct parallel occurred in the late 1980s when an equally supine British government sacked the cabinet minister Nicholas Ridley for suggesting that the European Union was merely a disguise for German national interests.

Those of us who have similarly not minced our words about the destruction of the British constitution since 1972 and have made comparisons with earlier attempts by a certain kind of German politician to dominate Europe, are frequently called "Germanophobes". Our analysis leads us to these conclusions not because we fear the Germans but because we know certain Germans. If we are "anti German" (the cry of the appeasers in the 1930s as today) then so was the former Chancellor Willy Brandt who left Germany in the 1930s, and fought (as "Herbert Fram") in the Norwegian resistance movement.

"Pro Germanism" was the characteristic of the 1930s appeasers and the post Second World War philosophy of the Pentagon's George Kennan who saw German rearmament as a bulwark against Soviet communism. John Major made much play, initially at least, of his "friend Helmut" even while the latter repeated many dangerous cliches of the 1930s. It was also the approach of the Bilderberg Group with its German former SS officer as founder (see chapter 7). Once again the parallels between pre-war appeasement and the post-war and present periods are clear. Even Gilbert and Gott's use of the term "sceptical" has its modern parallel: (16)

> "Pro Germanism began as an open and well argued attitude. But the more it was opposed and the more it was shown to

be inadequate if not erroneous the more it transformed itself into a *hidden obsession...* they began to *act behind closed doors* and to *scheme in the dark.* The public knew little of how appeasers acted before 1937; in the three years that followed they were to discover nothing at all."

I have emphasised the descriptions of the secrecy of appeasement since they accord so precisely with the habits of the Bilderberg Group and indeed the plans of Britain's major political parties as they have acted behind the backs of the electorate to surrender the British constitution and parliament to the new Eurostate.

If there is a modern equivalent to the conduct of Sir Samuel Hoare in Madrid, it is the conduct of Douglas Hurd at the Foreign Office, during the negotiations on the Maastricht Treaty and since he left office. It was Hurd who overturned John Major's promise not to proceed with the Maastricht Treaty if the Danish referendum rejected the treaty. The day before the vote Hurd effectively stabbed the Danish "No Campaign" in the back when he said that a "No" result would not after all mean that Britain would pull out of the treaty.

It was Hurd who showed his ignorance of elementary constitutional issues when he repeatedly claimed that a federal Europe would not be possible because the Union was a "decentralised" system, as if "federal" and "decentralised" were somehow opposites. The failure to distinguish between a British sovereignty and a foreign power would be ludicrous in an MP - it proved catastrophic in a Foreign Secretary.

It was Hurd who showed contempt for British democracy when, after a Government defeat over Maastricht, he pointed out what was tragically true - that "Parliament cannot overturn the Maastricht Treaty". On signing the Treaty (prior to any parliamentary consent) Hurd said "We had better go and read what we have signed".

Finally, after this track record of constitutional surrender, Hurd left the Government and became an employee of the Natwest

Bank - the driving force behind the "Association for Monetary Union in Europe" and whose former Chairman is prominent in the "Action Centre for Europe" which advocates the abolition of the Pound and the Bank of England. At some £200,000 per annum this move must be one of the best examples of political "contingent corruption" whereby politicians' actions in government are rewarded by those who benefit from them *after* the minister has left office. Douglas Hurd's activities in government were critical in the process of the European Union's takeover of the British judicial, political and economic system. Like Sir Samuel Hoare and his peerage, Hurd was awarded a "Companion of Honour", presented by the Sovereign he had helped to betray.

Once again Gilbert and Gott's words about 1930s appeasement could so easily apply to the new generation: (17)

> "It was the wise, the far sighted and the sceptical who talked of resisting Germany...Before 1937 appeasement was active at party and hunt. In 1937 it moved with Neville Chamberlain into 10 Downing Street. The vagaries of a mood became the realities of a policy."

Brought up to date the words might be:

> "Before 1990 appeasement was active in the Foreign Office (Howe and Hurd) and in the CBI. In 1990 it moved with John Major into 10 Downing Street, and 10 Downing Street moved into 'the heart of Europe'. The supranational plans of corporatism became the realities of constitutional betrayal."

(1) Martin Gilbert and Richard Gott *The Appeasers*, Weidenfeld and Nicholson, London 1963, page 37

(2) op cit page 37

(3) op cit page 38

(4) ibid

(5) op cit page 93

(6) op cit page 23

(7) op cit page 25

(8) op cit page 26

(9) *Kein Friede mit Deutschland*, Ulrich Schile, Langen Müller, Munich-Berlin 1994 (Bonn University doctoral thesis 1993). Page 296

(10) Gilbert and Gott page 50

(11) op cit page 45

(12) op cit page 133

(13) op cit page 69

(14) op cit page 132-33

(15) Schile, page 309

(16) Gilbert and Gott page 60

(17) ibid

11

THE POWER OF THE NAZI LEGACY

The European Union is based precisely on the social and economic structures of the "European Economic Community" proposed by the Hitler regime in 1941. The covert and undemocratic methods of forcing European Union rule on Britain - through Treaty law, directives and regulations which largely bypass parliament - had their equivalent in the emergency laws by which Hitler governed Germany.

None of this should surprise us, since the head of the "European Section" of the German Foreign Office in Adenauer's post-war government had held the same post under Hitler. 134 leading Nazi Foreign Office officials under Hitler were still in place in the early 1950s - until they were exposed by parliamentary questions.

I set out below how history has repeated itself. What the Nazis said and planned before, during and after the war, is now to be seen in the present activities of the German state, in the words of its leaders, in the philosophy of its collaborators in Belgium, Holland and France and in the power of the European Union, which Nazis designed and which "democratic" Germans and the heirs of Vichy France have forced on the once free peoples of Western Europe.

NAZI EUROPE	**TODAY'S "EUROPE"**
Czechoslovakia - a French aircraft carrier in the Middle of Europe (*Adolf Hitler*)	The status of the Czech republic has gone from that of a soviet satellite to that of a German protectorate (*The Prague Post*, 1996)
It is a question of German folk comrades! The Germans in Czechoslovakia are neither defenceless nor abandoned. Of that you can rest assured. (*Adolf Hitler, 1938*)	If European integration were not to progress, Germany might be called upon by its own security constraints to try to effect stabilisation of Eastern Europe in the traditional manner. (*German Christian Demcratic paper "Reflections on European Policy", 1995*)
...the longing for a 1000 year Reich cries for a new approach. For such a purpose we can use the mirage of a pan Europe. *(Dr Duisberg, I G Farben, 1931, Nazis' principal industrial ally, directors convicted at Nuremberg*)	The concept of European Unity is and remains the only effective insurance against nationalism. (*Helmut Kohl, December 1996*)
The world belongs to the man with guts. God helps him. (*Adolf Hitler in Joachim Fest, Hitler eine Biographe, Frankfurt, 1973, p. 683*)	Might is right in politics and war. (*Helmut Kohl, 1996*)

We are building the new Europe (Nazis as they marched into Norway)

The construction of the house of Europe remains the only real guarantee of freedom and peace in the 21st century. (*Helmut Kohl, 1996*)

In 1500 there was a German nation but no nationalism, whereas today when our eyes are supposed to light up at "Made in Germany" we have the reverse, nationalism and no nation. *Friedrich Reck-Malleczewen, 1937 Diary of a Man in Despair, Audiogrove 1995*

What does Europe therefore consist of? - Germany. *Konrad Adenauer*

The future will belong to the Germans when we build the house of Europe. *Helmut Kohl 1995*

"Our people have been sold into into the hands of international world capital. Do you want this to go on for ever? Then vote for the capitalist parties." *Nazi Party leaflet 1930s*

Deputy leader of the CDU parliamentary party, Heiner Geissler, claimed on record that capitalism was no better than communism. *Wall Street Journal, 28/4/1998*

Your actions played a significant role in our political struggle *Ante Pavelic, Croatian Fascist leader, speech to Catholic Action 21 June 1941*

"Genocide is a natural phenomenon, in harmony with the societal and mythological divine nature...it is not only permitted, it is recommended, even commanded by the Almighty." *Franjo Tudjman President of Croatia in Wastelands of Historical Reality, 1989*

German Secret Service under Franz Neuhausen active in Yugoslavia throughout 1930s plotting the country's break up.

German Intelligence Service under Klaus Kinkel from 1981 starts intensive campaign to undermine Yugoslavia. *E. Schmidt-Eenboom, Der Schattenkrieger, Econ Verlag, Dusseldorf 1997*

The papal legate in Croatia Mgr Marcone openly blessed the Ustasha and publicly gave the fascist salute.

In an official document dated May 8th 1944 His Eminence Archbishop Stepinac, head of the Catholic Hierarchy in fascist Croatia informed the Holy Father that to date "240,000 Orthodox Serbs have been converted to the Church of God." (FORCED CONVERSIONS) A. Manhattan, The Vatican's Holocaust, USA 1966

On 5th October 1998 the Pope makes the former Archbishop Stepinac of Croatia a saint.

"Kurt Waldheim is usually the only guest at the fund raiser for Friends of the Waffen SS" The Observer Magazine, 19/8/1988

1994 Waldheim receives a Knighthood from the Vatican.

In 1940s Yugoslavia the Nazis broke up the country into many racial and religious statelets. The German Waffen SS divisions were organised ethnically - Handzar - the Bosnian Muslims Kama - the Croats, Skenderbeg - the Albanians.

The first attempt to recreate a unit called "Handzar Division" was in Sisak, Croatia in the early 1990s.

More recently a Handzar division surfaced under the operational control of the Bosnian Government. One of its duties was to guard President Isetbegovic.

1940s Nazis drove most Serbs out of Kosovo, making them today a 10% minority in their own province where they were once the vast majority.

In 1996 the German Intelligence Services set up an operations centre in Tirana Albania, supplying weapons and communications equipment to the Kosovo "Liberation" Army.

What Germany needs is not Democracy but statecraft similar to the soviet dictatorship which enables the political elite in Germany to re-establish Europe as the power centre of the world. (*Nazi centre Madrid, 1950*)

Although heads of government have repeatedly called for more openness their declarations were of a political nature and therefore not binding on community institutions. (*European Court of Justice*)

The Germans alone can really organise Europe...Today we are practically the only power on the European mainland with a capacity for leadership. The Fuehrer is convinced that the Reich will be the master of all Europe. (*The Goebbels Diaries 1942-1943, New York 1948, p. 357)*

Look at Europe - what does it consist of? Britain? - aloof France? - politically unstable. Italy? - economically unstable And Benelux doesn't count. What does Europea therefore consist of? - Germany. *(Chancellor Konrad Adenauer quoted by Henry Brandon in his book The Retreat of American Power)*

Hitler said Czechoslovakia must in all be allied with Germany. He compared Czechs with "people who wanted to go to Nowawes but boarded the train for Grunau. They asked when the train would arrive at Potsdam and demanded that it should stop at Nowawes. They could not be made to understand that this was quite impossible, because the train did not go there. In Czechoslovakia they were also on the wrong train. They did not want to go in this direction but they had to because the points were set that way." (*Documents on German Foreign Policy 1919-1945. From the Archives of the German Foreign Office (Washington DC 1949) Series D no 158, p. 191, quoted in Gordon A. Craig, Germany 1866-1945, p. 705*)

Missing the European train.

We cannot go the speed of the slowest ship in the convoy. (*Helmut Kohl*)

Germany is the locomotive of the European train. (*Helmut Kohl*)

The continent is, with Germany and Italy, bound by fate. (*Nazi Prof. Heinrich Hunke, 1941*)

There is no alternative to a policy which aims at combination, unless we wish to challenge fate. (*Helmut Kohl, 1995*)

In his youth Hitler used to rub out Germany's borders in his school atlas.

As a young man Kohl got into trouble with the authorities for pulling down border markings on the French-German border.

To the architect of the New World Order, the protector of justice, our leader Adolf Hitler, as a token of gratitude and loyalty from the Croatian People, *Dr Anton Pavelic, Zagreb 2nd April 1941.*

"Danke, Deutschland"
Croatian Pop Song
1991

Democracy is a wishy washy word which has found no ear among the German people. (*Nazi propaganda Centre, Madrid, 1950*)

I never understood why public opinion about European ideas should be taken into account. (*Raymond Barre, former French Prime Minister*)

German democracy (is) characterised by election of a leader and his obligation fully to assume responsibility for his actions. In it there is no majority vote on individual questions but only the decision of an individual. *Hitler, Mein Kampf, Hutchinson, 1974, p. 83*

Dutch Reporter: "More than half the Dutch people want to keep the Guilder." Klaus Kinkel: "Then politicians should have the courage to take decisions if necessary against the will of the people." Reporter: "Excuse me?" Kinkel: "With the consent of Parliament of course."
NRC Handelsblad
31 January 1998

The Commons has never had power over European laws. When ministers go to Brussels they leave their democratic baggage behind them. *Bill Newton Dunn Tory MEP 1979-1994)*

On 24th March 1932 the Reichstag passed the Enabling Bill which allowed Hitler to draft and enact legislation without parliamentary approval.

European Policy has been conducted by a very small number of people - Kohl, Mitterand, Delors, two or three ministers; it's a very small circle where decisions are taken and then ratified *a posteriori*, with regrets about the democratic deficit. *Hubert Vedrine, chief adviser/negotiator to Mitterand at Maastricht*

We could never have constructed Europe by democratic means. (*Claude Cheysson, French Foreign Secretary*)

The Anglo-Saxon economic system, the classic national economy, is dead. (*Nazi Prof. Heinrich Hunke, 1941*)

It is important to establish a European Single Currency core in order to stand firm against Anglo-Saxon values. (*Philippe Maystadt, Belgian Finance Minister, 1996*)

Without France Europe will never equip itself with a single currency - more than ever the indispensable instrument with which to counter-balance the imperialism of the dollar."
Le Figaro 18th July 1997

Diaries of Sir Alexander Cadogan, May 1940: "Cartier (Belgian Ambassador) about 11 to protest against British troops going through Brussels, contrary to agreement. Said I was unaware of any agreement. Anyhow the essential was to get on the best defensive line to protect his beastly country."

In the Gulf War Belgium - a NATO ally - refused to sell ammunition to the United Kingdom.

Price stability in partner countries of Europe will permit less friction in currency relations. (*Nazi banker, Dr Bernhard Benning, 1941*)

The European Exchange Rate mechanism will provide currency stability in Europe. (*CBI*)

No Nation can achieve on its own the highest level of economic freedom compatible with all social requirements. *(Nazi economics Minister Walter Funk, 1941)*

The UK will join the single currency (ie abolish the pound) because the City wants it. *(Helmut Kohl)*

The UK must enter into the Single Currency (ie abolish the pound) if we wish to be rich and powerful. (*John Stevens, British MEP*)

We want an enclosed settlement in Europe. (*Nazi Prof. Heinrich Hunke, 1941*)

In order to save jobs in Europe it is the world that has to change. (*Le Figaro, 1995*)

...a world economy of the old style which is dependent on an overt or disguised Anglo-American world dominance. It is precisely because we want to prevent that that we are constructing a European block. (*Nazi Economics Minister Funk, 1941*)

The sovereignty of the nation state is a nineteenth century phenomenon *(Niall Fitzgerald, Chairman Unilever and CEI Europe Committee)*

There is no sense in putting together all European countries by means of a customs union in order to reconstruct for practical purposes a reduced form of the English world economy. (*Nazi Prof. Heinrich Hunke, 1941*)

We want the political union of Europe. Without monetary union there can be no political union and *vice versa.* (*Helmut Kohl*)

Defeats are simply lessons to be learned for the next attack .....the conquest of the world will require numerous stages. Each stage brings greater economic and industrial power... greater than our enemies.
Nazi General von Stuelpnagel 1944

Now we fly in the USA on a long term basis using our own German airplanes with our own German maintenance and instructors. It's *strictly national* training. *Lt Col Eckhard Sowada, Commander German Airforce at Holloman US Airforce base, New Mexico (home of Stealth bomber). No mention here of the end of narrow national sovereignty or of the "country called Europe"!*

Germany should "abandon all attempts at world industry and world trade and instead concentrate all her strength in order (to achieve) the allotment of sufficient living space for the next hundred years to our people ...Since this territory can only be in the East...Germany tries anew to champion her interests through the formation of a decisive power on land. (*Adolf Hitler, 1928, Adolf Hitler's Secret Book, New York, 1961, p. 142-145*)

Britain must be at the heart of Europe. (*John Major*)

Does free Europe want to join Germany? Germany is the heart of Europe and the limbs must adjust themselves to the heart not the heart to the limbs. (*Hans Seebohm Minister, Adenauer's Government, 1950*)

The French Government is bound to surrender on demand all German subjects designated by the Government of the Reich who are in France or in the French possessions... *Franco German Armistice Agreement 1940 Article 19*

All "European" citizens may at any time, without presentation in court of any *prima facie* evidence be arrested and taken to Germany for trial. But Germany has exempted itself from extraditing Germans on the same basis. *European Conventions on Extradition and (for the UK) 1989 Extradition Act*

We speak not of capital but of labour and that labour we employ to 100% effect. (*Adolf Hitler*)

Padraig Flynn, Europe's Social Affairs Commissioner, told the CBI conference that this (striking collective agreements) could take the initiative away from politicians and place it in the hands of management and labour. (*Evening Standard 8th November 1994*)

First give industry a large market for which to produce. That will be provided by the purchasing power of 300m united Europeans. Then *give industry a sure market* for which to produce ... Industry can then confidently install machinery and *mass* produce for a *large assured* market. (Italics show force of interventionist power of fascist State)
Oswald Mosley, Mosley Right or Wrong.

There is no possible way in which nation-states by themselves can adequately discipline let alone shape international economic forces; there is simply no alternative but to construct some supra-national arrangements which allow for a greater collective influence over at least our economic life.
Sir Leon Brittan, former sacked British Government Minister now Vice President, European Commission

Hitler, the eternal agitator, will not escape the necessity of acting. (*André François-Poncet, French ambassador in Berlin, 1933*)

If Germany puts forward clear and unequivocal proposals France must make equally clear decisions. France must rectify the impression...that it often hesitates in taking concrete steps towards this objective (*Paper issued by Christian Democratic Party, 1995*)

Hitler would be glad to suppress every copy of *Mein Kampf* extant today...Germany's *neighbours* have reason to be vigilant. (*Sir Horace Rumbold, 1939*)

On 15th December 1994, the *day the Swedish parliament ratified entry to the European Union*, the office of the publisher Haggland was was raided and copies of *Mein Kampf* confiscated. The State of Bavaria had obtained an injunction.

1936: Chamberlain took over from Baldwin, Halifax from Eden and Vansittart was sent to the Lords.

1938: Munich.

All effective propaganda must be limited to a few points and harp on these in slogans until the last member of the public understands what you want him to understand by your slogan. *Adolf Hitler, Mein Kampf, Hutchinson, 1934, page 164.*

The function of propaganda is not to weigh and ponder the rights of different people nor to make an objective study but to serve our own right, always and unflinchingly. *Adolf Hitler Mein Kampf page 166*

1990, Thatcher, Ridley and Lawson gave way to the policies of Major, Clarke and Hurd.

1992: Maastricht.

We must aim to shape public opinion...the general public is not yet sufficiently committed to the European ideal. *European Commission 9th General Report 1976*

It is judicious to act where resistance is weakest (to pro EU propaganda) *European Commission, de Clerq report 1993.*

We have commissioned research without it being seen to be Government inspired...it is important to ensure that not all results of opinion polls be in the public domain as some will be important to our cause and others will not. *1998 Labour Government's Northern Ireland Office (leaked) internal document on propaganda campaign to approve Northern Ireland Agreement.*

Today the British people have been turned into "citizens" of another country and their passports have been taken away (the one possession of "Lord Haw Haw" which proved his treason and led to his execution after the war). The borders of the United Kingdom can be crossed by any national of any member state of the EU, without question. Third country nationals must have visas to enter our country approved not by the British government but by the European Union. The laws of the British parliament can be overturned by a foreign court to which our own courts must look for superior judgement. All this has been achieved by a foreign power to which the British people hand over £8,000m per annum to finance a propaganda machine mobilised to destroy them.

Because Britain slept and some of its leading "democratic" politicians betrayed their country, the fascist agenda of the 1930s and 1940s is now almost complete. Even the excuse that, however similar modern Europe is to the Nazis' Europe, we could trust the democratic credentials of those who constructed it, cannot be credible when the "democratic" Chancellor of Germany can proclaim in 1996 that "Might is Right in politics and war".

In the 1930s the appeasers of Hitler and the dangerously naive called Churchill a "warmonger" and his supporters "Germanophobes". Similar accusations are heard today about opponents of a German-designed and dominated European Union. But those of us who have studied German politics and language and lived and worked in Germany do not fear Germans (who feel just as the British people) but we know certain Germans. We recognise that without a stable democratic, parliamentary or even national tradition the same German corporatist and anti-democratic forces which both led to and collaborated with the Hitler regime are once again driving Europe to disaster.

CONCLUSION

There was only one way that the forces which twice this century failed to create a European state under German domination could nevertheless achieve a similar aim by apparently peaceful means. There was only one way in which the power and influence of the British family of nations and the liberal trading order it represented could have been neutered while the political and economic power of Germany and its contiguous European "space" could have triumphed despite past defeats. There was only one way in which the "mother of parliaments" at Westminster could have lost all democratic power to a foreign bureaucracy. That one way was through the covert planning and ruthless implementation of a scheme to create a European Union, based on treaty laws rather than parliamentary sanction and framed in the manner of the American Union - *with neither provision nor mechanism for withdrawal.*

Just as in Germany in the 1920s the path was prepared by the creation of a state-dominated corporatist economy; just as in Germany in the 1930s "mass man" had been given political power by the weakening of the economic and moral leadership of individuals; as then, "mass man" is being mobilised in the only way possible, through collectivisation under state (and superstate) control.

The pattern of appeasement is virtually identical. Those who criticised the ever growing power of Nazi Germany and those who warn of a fascist Eurostate today were in both eras called "Germanophobe". While the Federation of British Industry collaborated with German industry even in 1939 the CBI today pours scorn on the right of the British people to a sovereign nation and parliament. While the broadcast media kept Churchill off the air from 1937 to 1939,[1] the anti-European Union movement was given precious little air time either before the passage of the Single European Act in 1986 or before the 1992-1993 Maastricht Treaty legislation. While the German people were only allowed to know what the Hitler regime "proposed" after it had carried it out, so the Maastricht Treaty was not published until after the 1992 election which, the British government claimed, had approved it.

While Churchill survived an attempt by Conservatives to deselect him in the late 1930s, the prominent Tory "Euro-sceptic" Sir George Gardiner faced a similar threat (which he comfortably survived) in 1996. While Rudolf Hess, having parachuted into Scotland in 1941, demanded the resignation of Churchill, so the Bilderberg Group in 1989 seems to have "discussed" the resignation of Margaret Thatcher, the Euro-fanatics' greatest opponent. While Sir Samuel Hoare, arch-appeaser of the 1930s and ambassador in Spain from 1940 to 1944 plotted with the German circle around Hess to remove Churchill, today Sir Leon Brittan, one of our "Commissioners" in Brussels, daily defies his oath of allegiance to the United Kingdom and directs policies against subjects of the Queen in Canada.

Brittan's fellow Irish Commissioner, Padraig Flynn, recommends in public what Hitler so effectively achieved - that corporations should bypass national parliaments and do what the unelected Brussels Commission advises. The leader of the British "Liberal" Party fawns on the new Eurostate just as Liberals like Lord Lothian and Lloyd George fawned on Hitler. While Rudolf Hess demanded to speak to "The King's Party", Chancellor Helmut Kohl acquires power over the British people through the use of "Crown Prerogative" and pontificates from Bonn that the British Pound will be abolished "because the City wants it".

The same international corporatist plans which made Hitler's life so easy are now being realised, often under the same cliches - "European integration", "new world order", "heart of Europe" and "international solidarity". There is hardly a single element of the European Union which was not planned by the

Nazis in 1942 and hardly any aspect of the Nazi condemnation of free trade and the "Anglo Saxon System" which is not repeated in Brussels, Bonn and Paris today, albeit *sotto voce*.

This book has shown how many key figures in British politics have promoted the destruction of the nations of Europe while accepting honours bestowed by those nations. Some like Heath plotted from within, others like the Eurocrat and Hitler appeaser Denman[2] or Lord Jenkins acted from their European Community-funded positions outside, while others like Toynbee with positions in the British academic and civil service Establishment, showed in covert circles their contempt for the nation which they "served".

Throughout the 1920s and the 1930s Germany established a State-dominated corporatist conservatism to which all major parties subscribed, even as unemployment rose to such levels that the Nazi and Communist parties flourished. Today the British Conservative Party, having been abandoned by individual Conservatives has relied on the donations of large corporations which have therefore largely dictated the legislative programme - not least on Europe. While Conservative Party individual membership halved, a Party deficit of £19m was turned into a surplus of £20m, through largely undisclosed corporate donations. Both Labour and Liberal Parties have joined the new "Conservative Party" in its pursuit of anti-democratic corporatism. Liberals are prepared to sacrifice all vestiges of a liberal constitution in the name of a bureaucratic Eurostate. The Labour Party are prepared to sacrifice for ever their rights to make social and industrial policy, even if it is conducted instead by a fascist Eurostate to which the Maastricht Treaty commits them "irrevocably and irreversibly". Major and Blair seek to outbid each other in their corporatist cliches ("UK plc", "stakeholders") and rush to buy votes with the proceeds of privatised monopolies and a nationalised lottery run for private profit.

The collectivised mass is encouraged to spend in consumerist hedonism the capital previously accrued and managed wisely by the few. The collective corporations are balanced by collective unions and - as in 1920s Germany - by a few associations of privileged consumers. Free and responsible individuals, families and communities are left out in the cold, unable to coerce either the economic or political sources of power. What has happened to these honourable institutions of a free society is now happening to nations themselves.

Europe has come full circle. The United Kingdom faces the same political crisis as in the 1930s. We have a choice between on the one hand appeasement of supranational corporatism and an imperialist continental power built on the *suppression* rather than the *expression* of public opinion and on the other hand the British family of nations with its open world wide trading system and rule of law by which our country has maintained the loyalty of those we once ruled and which continues to attract the world's free nations. I hope this book may help to reverse the present tragic course of events and by retrieving the self government of our nation, we may save Europe by our example.

(1) Even in the BBC's German language broadcasts a programme of "views" called *Sonderbericht* attempted no political objectivity. Asa Briggs in his *History of Broadcasting in the UK Vol II* (page 649) noted that up to March 1939, "...the content of the *Sonderbericht* service was consistent with a continuing policy of appeasement."

(2) Sir Roy Denman was part of the UK's EEC negotiating team from 1970 to 1972, Director General of External Affairs from 1977 to 1982 and then the European Community's "ambassador" to the USA. He not only attacked Churchill but opposed Britain's entry into the war against Hitler. By allowing the Russians to destroy Hitler, he wrote in his recent book *Missed Chances* (Cassell, 1996), "It would have been a very different world. Britain, France and the Low Countries would have remained intact." This farcical theory might have had more credibility had not Hitler conquered France two years before declaring war on Russia! But such are the theories of those British failures whom the party Establishments have habitually sent to "Europe" and adorned with knighthoods.

Appendix I

BRITAIN AND "EUROPE": A CONSTITUTIONAL AND ECONOMIC DISASTER

As we have seen in earlier chapters the socio-economic fascism of continental Europe under German influence is diametrically opposed to everything that Anglo Saxon liberal internationalism represents. It is also clear that the violent, abusive and illiberal language of the chief proponents of an "integrated Europe", both in the United Kingdom and on the Continent, suggests that any system which they might construct is going to be the antithesis of any parliamentary system which we would deem democratic.

It is also evident that the British economy, for centuries used to free international trade, market pricing and a domestic market open to foreign competition will have suffered untold damage after 24 years exposed to the "Continental" system so beloved of Vichy France, Nazi Germany and Fascist Italy and largely reproduced in today's European Union.

The way in which the "European" Union has arbitrarily imposed a world-wide export ban on British beef without a single piece of scientific evidence and in the face of British, European and World Health Organisation expert opinion that our beef is safe, demonstrates beyond doubt that the United Kingdom is now powerless to prevent total control of our economy and political institutions by a foreign power, consisting largely of those very countries which between 1939 and 1945 spread their fascist doctrine to every corner of continental Europe. And all this has been done under Treaties freely signed by Conservative Government ministers, passed by our Parliament and implemented by our judicial system (because our judges have no choice).

This scandalous betrayal of everything for which two generations of Britons gave their lives in two wars was covertly agreed and unconstitutionally bulldozed through Parliament. The chief pillars of the British constitution were swept away not by explicit, overt laws democratically discussed, but by implied repeal - that is surreptitiously, without expressly stating to the Houses of Parliament or the British people that historic statutes and case law were in fact being destroyed by European Treaties, signed by ministers under "Crown Prerogative". This is perhaps the most despicable aspect of a process of destruction by a "Conservative" government which will live in infamy.

During the passage of the 1972 European Communities Act the then Conservative government assured the British people that they were joining a **common market of sovereign nation states**. From comments he has made since we now know that the then Prime Minister, Edward Heath, was always prepared to accept the loss of our national sovereignty for the sake of a European superstate. Legislation in 1972, 1986 (Single European Act) and 1993 (Maastricht) has ensured that his intentions are being fulfilled.

The European Union has 15 member states. But Europe consists of 42 countries and the three richest countries according to UN statistics published in 1993 were Switzerland, Norway and Sweden — **not one of which was then a member of the European Community**. In order to persuade the Swedes to vote 52% to 48% in favour of joining the EU, the Swedish government used taxpayers' money to spend 20 times the funds available to the "No" campaign.

When the people of Norway and Switzerland **rejected** European Union membership their currencies and stock markets rose and interest rates fell. As the *Financial Times* noted, **"independence pays dividends"**. Today there are large majorities against EU membership in Norway, Sweden and Austria.

The historical strength of Europe has been in the stability and inheritance of its **nations**. Not one single significant achievement in Europe — and certainly not the defeat of German Imperialism and National Socialism in two wars — was ever achieved by supranational powers. Either individual nations acted alone or countries formed **alliances between** sovereign nations.

Only since the "Common Market" developed into a "European Community", with political systems and legal power to override national democracies, has Europe failed economically (poor growth and investment), socially (highest and longest-term unemployment in the advanced countries), and politically (increasing tensions between European countries and increased power for fascist parties in Germany, France and Italy).

HOW "EUROPE" DESTROYED THE BRITISH CONSTITUTION

The "European" legislation of 1972, 1986 and 1993 (swept through the British Parliament on a tide of ignorance, and intimidation of MPs) was based on two unprecedented constitutional procedures:

1. the use of **international treaties** to negotiate the **internal constitution** of the United Kingdom.
2. the **general** transfer by our Parliament of powers to the "European" Community which then legislates **specifically** within the United Kingdom by Directive and Regulation which the British parliament is powerless to resist.

The transfer of GENERAL powers to the state to act without the sanction of parliament is precisely how Adolf Hitler gained such absolute power through his emergency laws.

Since 1972 the British people have lost:

- the unrestricted right of our parliament to make the laws in our country. (The European Court of Justice has suspended laws passed by our own MPs.)
- the supreme right of the British courts to interpret and uphold the law. (British judges must now refer to the European Court in Luxembourg.)
- the British passport. (The traditional passport has been replaced by a "European" passport.)
- the right NOT to be a citizen of another state without our consent. We have been made "European Citizens" with "duties" (as yet undefined) towards the European Union.
- our sovereign Queen who has been turned into a "European Citizen", also with duties to and taxable by the European Union. The Queen is therefore now in a position not of sovereignty but of **suzerainty**.
- the exclusive right to decide through the UK parliament their own taxes. It is now illegal for Britain to reduce below 15% VAT already applied to goods and services at that rate or more.
- because of the introduction of new areas of EU majority voting, our parliament can be outvoted in every policy area except foreign affairs, the budget, defence and (some) social policies. But Maastricht says even this veto right "should not be used".
- the right to judicial arbitration by a non-political court. The overriding **"European Court of Justice" is a political court devoted, in its own words, to "overcoming the resistance of national governments to European integration".**
- the right to be governed only by policies put forward by British political parties. Today policies are enacted which

were never mentioned in British party manifestos nor discussed or approved in the British parliament.

- the right to our internationally recognised fishing grounds in our 200 mile territorial waters. Even the British EC fishing quota can now be bought by, for example, Spanish fishermen. The European Community recently handed over to Spanish fishermen the right to fish off the South West of Britain. The British minister was powerless to stop this. A recent UN report on fishing conservation said that **national government** control had proved the best. They particularly mentioned the Falkland Islands - where the British government enjoys the sovereignty it has lost at home.

- the right to control our borders and the right to decide who can work, reside and vote in the UK. These are automatically the rights of all "European citizens", **who can be created by each member state simply by making anyone into a national of that country.**

- (from 1996) the right to decide who from non-EU countries (e.g. the Commonwealth or the USA) can have a visa to enter the UK.

- the right to the exclusive hallmarking of gold and silver under our 700-year-old, internationally recognised hallmarking laws. In future we must accept a Euro-hallmark covering inferior standards across the EU.

- the UK's right to check, control and quarantine imported farm animals at our borders. Now they can only be inspected at the farm — when it is often too late. As a result at least two British prize herds have been wiped out.

- British subjects who have sworn allegiance to the Queen but are now employed as European "Commissioners" and "Ambassadors" recently, in the name of Europe and the British people, attacked Canada and the Canadian people who are fellow subjects of the Queen and whom the British people wholeheartedly support. **The UK Government said nothing.**

This unprecedented loss of sovereignty has occurred without the consent of the British people. Over £20,000m of British taxpayers' money in net budget contributions have financed EU propaganda. In Britain, the Government gave £10,000 to the pro-Euro-federalist "European Movement" because it is a "cross-party organisation" but no such money was granted to any anti-European "cross-party organisation".

THE MASSIVE ECONOMIC COSTS OF "EUROPE"

- In 22 years of membership of the European Community the UK has paid net budget contributions of £25,000m to be a member of a club with which we have accumulated a **visible** trade deficit of £100,000m.

- In 1994 the UK paid £7.4 *billion* gross to the EU budget but only £2.37 million to the "General Agreement on Tariffs and Trade" (GATT) the world-wide organisation for international trade.

- Between 1973 and 1993 the UK's **total** trade deficit with the EC was £70,000m but the UK had a **surplus** over that period with the rest of the world of £80,000m. British withdrawal from the EU might be a threat to "Europe", but certainly not to the UK.

- Although the UK gets 43% of its overseas earnings from the EU, such trade accounts for 75% of all our trading deficit — **despite EU countries taking the largest share of our North Sea oil.**

- In 1973 the UK left EFTA to join the EEC. **By 1994 every single member of EFTA was richer than every member of the EEC except Luxembourg.**

- When Britain joined the EEC it was the third richest member state and the second richest member of EFTA.

Today we are the fourth poorest in the EU and poorer than all EFTA members.

- Britain is nevertheless the 2nd biggest contributor to the EU budget. The present contribution of £7,000m per annum will rise by 1997 to £10,000m per annum. Although some of this vast sum is returned to the UK, **its use is decided by the European Community, not by the elected British government.**

- the large blue signs erected by the European Community at the road-side of some project which Europe claims to have "funded" are blatant, empire-building propaganda and a lie. "Funded" means they LENT us the money! IF actual grants were made the British people paid for those grants plus 50% more — wasted in EU bureaucracy.

- A Northern Ireland project, "funded" by the EC, did not display the Euroflag with the EC's claim to have "funded" the project. The company was told by EC officials that they would have a better chance of future "help" only if such a Euro-poster were erected!

- membership of the **EU has nothing to do with our ability to trade with the EU**. Switzerland, neither an EU member nor even associated with the "European Economic Area", exported per capita in 1993 three and a half times as much to the EU as Britain. Norway exported three times as much and Sweden (then outside the EU) twice as much as Britain.

- the Confederation of British Industry and government ministers frequently lie about the importance of the EU for Britain, pretending for instance that the Japanese would not invest here if we were not in the EU. But Japanese companies also invest heavily in Hungary which is not an EU member and have **repeatedly said that British EU membership is irrelevant to their investment decisions, recently even saying they would regard a European**

Single Currency as a problem for their investments in Britain.

- 75% of our overseas investment is **outside** the EU. We are the world's largest investor in the world's largest economy — the USA.

- We receive nearly twice as much investment income from the Commonwealth as from the European Union.

- hundreds of thousands of British jobs have been lost in shipbuilding, fishing, coal, airlines, computers and steel because commercial British companies cannot compete with massive state subsidies for these industries in France, Germany, Italy and Spain — all approved by the European Council of Ministers, **in which British Ministers are outvoted**.

- long-term unemployment in the EU at 46% of the unemployed is far worse than in the USA (7%) and Japan (18%).

- the European Union has a far worse record than either the USA or Japan on employment costs, productivity growth, investment and inflation.

- Europe is the only continent with which Britain has a trade deficit.

- the British family of four pays £28 per week (£1,500 per year) more for food in the European Community than we would if buying on world markets.

- British farmers only produce 70% of the milk needed by the British people. Europe's Common Agricultural Policy prevents them from producing any more so we *have* to import from other member states with higher-cost producers.

- When the Federation of Small Businesses asked their members what had been the chief result of the UK's membership of the EU, 60% replied "increased legislation and administrative costs" (only 5% mentioned increased sales.)

- Joining a Single European Currency would mean abolishing the Pound Sterling and the Bank of England. All Bank of England reserves would be handed over to the European Central Bank in Germany and all Britain's foreign exchange earnings (£79,000 million per annum) would benefit the Euro-state and its Single Currency.

- When the Chairmen of the top 100 British companies were asked by the *Sunday Telegraph* whether their company was a) British b) international c) European or d) global, **most said British, none said European.**

CONCLUSION

Never in the history of the British Nation have so much constitutional power and so many parliamentary rights been sacrificed to such disastrous economic effect.

If our nation, our 800-year-old parliament and our peaceful and tolerant society are to survive, we must withdraw immediately from the European Union and restore our self- government and trading freedom in the "European Economic Area" — today's equivalent to the "Common Market" which the British people accepted at the 1975 referendum.

Appendix II

THE CONSERVATIVE PARTY AND THE EUROPEAN CRISIS

The following MPs have shown that they understand the constitutional crisis into which the United Kingdom has been plunged by its membership of the European Union. The most reliable are in bold script! However even these MPs must be asked to clarify where they stand on the reclaiming of our national right to self government - that is the repeal of most of the European legislation which has destroyed our democratic constitution and parliamentary rights.

MP	**Constituency**
John Redwood	Wokingham
Michael Clark	Rochford
Christopher Gill	**Ludlow**
Sir Teddy Taylor	**Southend East**
Ann Winterton	Congleton
Sir Richard Body	**Holland with Boston**
James Cran	**Beverley**
Teresa Gorman	**Billericay**
David Porter	Waveney
Michael Spicer	Worcestershire South
Nicholas Winterton	**Macclesfield**
Bill Cash	**Stafford**
Iain Duncan Smith	**Chingford**
Richard Shepherd	**Aldridge Brownhills**
Sir Peter Tapsell	Lindsey East
John Wilkinson	**Ruislip Northwood**
Edward Leigh	**Gainsborough & Horncastle**
Bernard Jenkin	Colchester North

John Whittingdale	Colchester South & Malden
John Townend	Bridlington
Rhodes Boyson	Brent North
Gerald Howarth	Aldershot
Dr Julian Lewis	New Forest East
Oliver Letwin	West Dorset

The following are not in the present parliament but could be regarded as Eurosceptic enough to be re-selected in future:

John Biffen	Toby Jessel
John Butcher	Sir Mark Lennox Boyd
Tony Marlow	Walter Sweeney
Roger Knapman	Warren Hawkesley
Sir Trevor Skeet	Sir Gerard Vaughan
John Carlisle	Rupert Allason
Barry Legg	Sir George Gardiner
David Parker	Vivian Bendall
Bill Walker	Sir Ivan Laurence

Even those who seem to have understood the crisis and could in general be called "eurosceptic" must show continuously that they are fighting in parliament to leave the European Union's constitutional clutches and to return us to that common market of self governing nations which the peoples of Europe want and which the British people voted for in the 1975 referendum (but did not get).

Nearly all other Conservative MPs, including those who are members of the Government cannot be trusted even to understand never mind to defend our national independence, the sovereignty of our parliament or the self government of our democracy.

Either they understood what the European Legislation of 1972, 1986, 1993 and 1997 (Amsterdam Treaty) meant for the British Constitution in which case they deliberately disguised this from the electors and betrayed their country;

Or they failed to even read or having read were incapable of understanding the disgraceful legislation which gave away the democratic rights of the British people.

There is of course a chance that they will see the error of their ways - especially when reminded of the strength of feelings of the electorate! In any case they must be required to reply with the right answers to the questions below.

QUESTIONS FOR YOUR MP OR PROSPECTIVE CANDIDATE

Q: Do you understand that the only mandate that any Government has had from the people of Britain was for a Europe of sovereign (ie self governing) nations co-operating and trading freely with each other?

A: Yes.

Q: Then why did you support the 1986 Single European Act and the Maastricht Treaty legislation?

A: Because I was foolish. I now regret my actions and I will campaign to reverse the elements in those Acts which prohibit the absolute excercise of self government by the Westminster Parliament and it is the real Europe of the other 32 countries which Britain must join and lead.

Q: If we have a VAT rate on any goods or services in the United Kingdom of 17.5% and our parliament wishes to reduce it to 10% or abolish it altogether, can we do so ?

A: NO - it is illegal under the laws of the European Union.

Q: Did you realise that only a temporary exemption from an EU directive allows the UK NOT to put VAT on childrens' cloths, food and books? What do you intend to do about this?

A: Yes, I realise that if we don't leave the EU we cannot decide for ourselves which goods will attract VAT.

Q: Do you understand that even the 1972 European Act destroyed the sovereignty of the British nation, the British parliament and the British people and that the Single European Act and Maastricht Treaty made the situation even worse?

A: Yes.

Q: Do you understand that the richest countries in Europe - Norway, Switzerland and Liechenstein - are not and never have been in the European Union and that the European Union only represents one third of the countries of Europe?

A: Yes.

Q: Do you realise that the European Court, which daily makes laws for the British people without consulting our parliament and which has suspended laws passed by our parliament is not a normal court at all but one which has a mission (in its own words) "to promote European Integration".

A: Yes.

Q: What percentage of our fish stocks in our internationally recognised territorial waters did we give up to the European Union in 1972?

A: 70%.

Q: Do you know what the cumulative manufacturing trade deficit with the European Union has been since 1973?

A: About £150,000 million.

Q: Do you know how much in net contributions to the European Budget Britain has payed since 1973?

A: About £30,000 million.

Q: This year we will make net contributions to the EU budget of about £3,500 million. The world Organisation for free trade between the nations is called the GATT. Do you know how much we pay to that Organisation each year?

A: £2.3 million.

Q: How much does a British family of four pay extra for food from the European Union because of its Common Agricultural policy?

A: £28 per week.

Q: What does the European Single Currency mean for the Pound Sterling and the Bank of England?

A: The abolition of both which means the end of British national self government.

Q. Do you realise that the EURO means the end of the Pound and the end of the Pound means the end of Britain?

A. Yes - there has never been a democratic self governing nation without its own currency.

Q: Of every Pound which the United Kingdom receives from the European Union how much have we already payed in?

A: About £2.

Q: The British Passport in its traditional form has been abolished. In which of our party's manifestos was this policy mentioned? Will you vote for the return of the original British passport in style AND CONTENT?

A: It was not mentioned at all. I will vote for the return of the traditional passport.

Q: Not long ago we told the Australian and New Zealand people (through the Spanish Foreign Minister representing the European Union) that they were "stupid and ignorant" to criticise France's nuclear tests in the South Pacific. What complaint did you make to our Government about this? What was the result? What do you intend to do about it?

A: I thought it was disgraceful. I complained to the PM. I will vote to prevent the European Union making our foreign policy for us.

Q: Will you agree to vote in Parliament to return the United Kingdom to the constitutional position the British people thought they had agreed to in 1975? Will you vote to leave the European Union and become a member of the European Economic Area - that is economically associated with the European Union, trading freely with it but otherwise deciding all economic, political, social and foreign policies exclusively in our own parliament and living freely under our 800 year old constitution?

A: Yes

Q. Do you agree to resign immediately from this parliamentary seat if you go back on any of these answers and if this constituency votes to remove you as our MP?

A. I solemnly swear to do so.

Appendix III

THE LABOUR PARTY AND THE EUROPEAN CRISIS

Like the other major political parties in the United Kingdom the new Labour Party leadership has somehow got the impression that the "European Union" is the same thing as Europe. In fact, of course, of the 45 countries in Europe only 15 are in the European Union.

Indeed the three richest countries in Europe - Norway, Switzerland and Liechtenstein - are not (nor have they ever been) in the European Community. They are still sovereign countries, governed by their own parliaments, in which their courts of law cannot be overruled by the "European Court of Justice", whose agriculture and fishing industries are not run by Brussels and whose foreign trade, foreign policy and defence are not compromised by a foreign power. In short, they still have that for which two generations of British people fought and died in two world wars.

Labour opposed Britain's membership of the Common Market and then of the European Community until 1985. Only since Europe's power to control our country and parliament reached unprecedented levels in the late 1980s did the Labour party change its policy and agree, by their support for the Maastricht Treaty, effectively to surrender the British government's right to govern Britain.

THE SOCIAL CHAPTER

The very party which, since its foundation in the early years of this century, has concentrated on social affairs, trade union and employment law is now prepared to give up its power to make policy in these areas. As soon as Labour comes to power it will hand over "irrevocably and irreversibly", as the Treaty says, all these policy areas to the European Union - **over which the British people and parliament have no control whatsoever.**

The Maastricht Treaty is a constitutional treaty not a cooperation agreement. The new Labour Party seems to think it could sign up to the Social Chapter but only implement those policies which it wanted. It would of course have no such choice. On every single issue Labour would be outvoted by other countries in the Council of Ministers. **Tony Blair has not yet explained why, if he forms the next British Government, he should not then pass the labour laws he wants, without joining the Social Chapter.**

What if the increasing success of the Neo-Nazis in Germany, the National Front in France and the Neo-Fascists in Italy led to their controlling the European Council of Ministers and the European Commission? The Labour leadership appears to believe this doesn't matter - they will do ("irrevocably and irreversibly") whatever a majority of EU members vote for. Indeed they even support extending the areas in which majority voting is applied.

MAASTRICHT ECONOMICS

Having wholeheartedly supported the Maastricht Treaty the Labour Party has committed itself to the economic "convergence criteria" which means fines could be imposed on a Labour government by the European Union if these criteria were not met. If the UK is so poor it cannot meet the convergence criteria it will of course be greatly helped by paying fines to Brussels!

But here at least there are signs of doubt for in February 1996 the Labour Party front bench voted against (and defeated) the Government on the Maastricht convergence criteria. At last the Labour Party leadership seems to be waking up to what they have been doing by slavish devotion to the "European" Union. It is a pity that it is too late to change the "irrevocable and irreversible" Maastricht Treaty which lays down the convergence criteria which Labour now seems to oppose.

THE BRITISH CONSTITUTION

With a few principled exceptions (see list) the new "social democrat" Labour Party has *kowtowed* to the new Eurofascism and repeatedly voted for the same method of destroying parliamentary democracy used by Adolf Hitler. Without specifically destroying the German constitution Hitler used his emergency laws to rule by decree. They allowed him to bypass parliament and impose his rule without reference to parliamentary debate or approval.

British Conservative governments, in signing the Treaties of Rome and Maastricht, used the powers of Treaty Law to sign away the democratic rights of the British people. As Douglas Hurd said when the Government was defeated on a Maastricht vote: **"It doesn't matter - the House has no power to overturn the Maastricht Treaty"**. How true.

The Labour Party has in fact criticised Prerogative Powers in one of its policy statements: *"It is where power is exercised by government under cover of royal prerogative that our concerns are greatest"*. Not apparently so great as to vote against the scandalous use of those very powers in the Maastricht Treaty which destroyed the parliamentary rights of Labour MPs and voters.

Equally anti-democratic is how an international treaty gave *general* powers to a foreign institution (the European Commission) to make *specific* laws (directives and regulations) in the United Kingdom which the British parliament is powerless to reject, or indeed often even to debate. This is the essence of fascism - the power of the state to bypass parliament and the will of the people. The Labour Party leadership voted for it.

The Labour Party is to offer a referendum to the Scots on devolution and to the British electorate on voting by proportional representation in the United Kingdom, having opposed a referendum on Maastricht to decide what powers our parliament should have. Not until the 1997 election did they commit to a referendum on the abolition of the Pound.

PARTY LEADERSHIP'S NAIVETY ON EUROPE

The new Labour Party has just been found guilty in the British courts for using women-only shortlists for selecting candidates to fight parliamentary seats. It has had to discontinue this discriminatory policy.

But a slight knowledge of what was going on in Europe would have told them that the German Christian Democrats had a similar policy towards women candidates, were taken to the European Court and told the policy was illegal. So even if Labour (as they say they want to) were to change the law in this country they would be overruled by the European Court of Justice.

The "New Labour" party is equally naive when they support a single European currency - that is, the abolition of the Pound and the Bank of England. They will accept an independent (and highly monetarist) central bank based in Frankurt while they reject an independent central bank (and *all* monetarist policies) in the United Kingdom.

Chancellor Kenneth Clarke displayed his anti-democratic credentials when he said about the European Community:

> **"The good thing about Europe is that it makes most of the Labour Party's policies illegal."**

How right he was - and how easily the "moderate" leadership of the new Labour Party has been duped by "Europe".

COMMISSIONER KINNOCK AND BRITISH JOBS

The former leader of the Labour Party, Neil Kinnock, is the European Commissioner responsible for transport policy. He approved a massive grant of aid by the Spanish government to Iberia, the Spanish airline, in 1995 on various conditions including that this would be the last injection of funds. British workers in profitable, unsubsidised airlines like Air UK, British Airways or British Midland, had to pay the price in lost business and lost jobs.

A year later Mr Kinnock agreed another "final" injection into Iberia. No matter how much European Commissioners like Kinnock and Brittan may try to stop these unfair, job-destroying subsidies, *we will be outvoted by those governments like the French, the German, the Italian and the Spanish who always subsidise their car, airline, computer, shipbuilding and many other industries - all at the cost of British workers' jobs.* And this is the system which Tony Blair is going to "influence".

WHAT CAN LABOUR SUPPORTERS DO?

Labour supporters must rescue their country, their parliament and their democracy by supporting candidates who oppose the European Union. Conservatives in constituencies where the Conservative candidate is unacceptable might also wish to identify anti-EU Labour candidates. Here is a list of the Labour MPs who can be (more or less) trusted to oppose the new Eurofascism:

LABOUR

Diane Abbot	Hackney North and Stoke Newington
Roger Berry	Kingswood
Ronnie Campbell	Blythe Valley
Denis Canavan	Falkirk West
Denzil Davies	Llanelli
Mildred Gordon	Bow and Poplar

Terry Lewis	Worsley
Ted Rowlands	Merthyr Tydfil and Rhymney
George Stevenson	Stoke on Trent South
Harry Cohen	Leyton
Gwynneth Dunwoody	Crewe and Nantwich
Alan Simpson	Nottingham South
Audrey Wise	Preston
Tony Benn	Chesterfield
John Cummings	Easington
Dr John Gilbert	Dudley East
Austin Mitchell	Great Grimsby
Dennis Skinner	Bolsover
Jimmy Wray	Glasgow, Provan
Michael Clapham	Barnsley West
Llew Smith	Blaenau Gwent
Andrew Bennet	Denton
John Austin Walker	Woolwich
Bill Michie	Sheffield Heely
David Winnick	Walsall North
Ken Purchase	Wolverhampton North East
Ann Cryer	Keighley
John Cryer	Hornchurch

No MP can be trusted as a democratic representative unless he accepts (at least) the return to that association with "Europe" which the (deceived) British people thought they were agreeing to in 1975 - i.e. an economic and cooperative agreement between sovereign nations. Many will of course reject even that. But no MP who supports the **actual** loss of our democratic rights since the 1972 European Act and certainly no MP who supports the present European Union is acceptable.

The one way democrats can defeat the anti-democratic party hierarchies and their fellow travellers in the media is to circulate leaflets **which do no more than tell the truth** about the constitutional and democratic destruction of our country.

A PLEA TO THE READER OF THIS BOOK

It is precisely the kind of collectivist and corporatist society here described which makes the publication and sale of this book (written by an individual who is independent of any corporation or state institution and published by a small publisher) a difficult enterprise.

We have limited resources to promote and sell it through the usual commercial outlets, or the "clout" to have it reviewed in national newspapers and periodicals. Although this has not prevented successful sales of other books by the author, we believe that, such is the critical importance of this book for the future of the British nation and parliament, we must rely to a great extent on the initiative of individual readers.

Lobbying of newspapers, magazines, journalists, politicians, book buyers and libraries will all help to put the warnings in this book before a wider audience. The European Union spends £200 million per annum on "information" and "promotion". The author and publisher would be most grateful for your help in our attempts to counter such official, tax-funded propaganda.

We earnestly hope that our efforts will help return to our nation the democracy and self-government for which generations of Britons have fought and died.

COMMENTS ON RODNEY ATKINSON'S OTHER PUBLICATIONS

"Excellent, fascinating"
Nobel Laureate Milton Friedman

"In the UK Gas market as in other areas Rodney Atkinson has proved to be a visionary."
Sir James MacKinnon
Director General, Office of Gas Supply.

"Very good indeed, I commend it strongly"
Rt Hon David Howell MP Former Secretary of State for Energy and Chairman, House of Commons Foreign Affairs Select Committee.

"I am very much in agreement"
Sir Alan Walters, Adviser to Prime Minister Margaret Thatcher

"Brilliant"
Professor Norman Barry, University of Buckingham

"Rodney Atkinson's real interest proposal deserves very serious consideration."
Professor Patrick Minford, University of Liverpool

"A powerful argument"
Dr John Gray, Oxford University

"If the Government wants to know what needs to be done Ministers should read Rodney Atkinson's pamphlet."
Professor Norman Stone, Oxford University

"A unique and refreshing defence of liberty"
Laissez Faire Books, New York.

"A devastating analysis of the costs and effects of regional policy"
London Evening Standard

"Closely and cleverly reasoned"
Matthew Parris of The Times

"Atkinson's latest box of intellectual fireworks."
Lord Harris of High Cross

"Excellent, devastating"
George Gilder, Author "Wealth and Poverty"

"As acute, witty and well documented as ever"
Encounter

"A breath of fresh air"
Petroleum Economist

"An admirable analysis of a deep international problem."
Lord Pennock, CBI

"Brilliantly argued"
FT Energy Economist

"I found a great deal with which I agree, particularly in the analysis of what needs to be done and still has not been done."
Rt Hon Keith Joseph MP

"An excellent book"
Sunday Times

"Extremely well argued and lucidly written."
Professor Norman Barry, University of Buckingham

"I congratulate you on your endeavours and warmly welcome your paper. It represents a stimulating contribution to the regional policy debate."
Sir Giles Shaw MP, Minister of State, Department of Trade & Industry.

"Mr Atkinson's onslaught shows how far this or any other Government is from applying sensible market principles."
Samuel Brittan, Financial Times

"An eloquent analysis"
British Petroleum executive.

TREASON AT MAASTRICHT
THE DESTRUCTION OF THE NATION STATE

Rodney Atkinson and Norris McWhirter

ISBN 0 9509353 9 5 Paperback 1997 Price £8.00

How the British constitution was destroyed on the altar of a European State designed by the Nazis in 1942 to defeat "Anglo Saxon democracy" and liberal world trade.

"In our fight for freedom your book was a cruise missile which I hope is still finding targets"

Vice Admiral Sir Louis le Bailly, former Director General, Defence Intelligence Staff

"(British Commissioners in Brussels) should bear allegiance to one or other but not both sovereigns"

A former Lord of Appeal in ordinary

"I agree and have bought more copies to circulate among other judges"

High Court Judge

"Powerful Stuff!"

Bill Jamieson, The Sunday Telegraph

"Two latter day St Georges slashing to pieces the myths and lies woven around 'Europe'"

This England Magazine

OTHER READERS

"I must congratulate you on your absolutely splendid and revealing work ... without its success our country is in the most deadly peril" **Brian Coventry**. "Very well done - it should be circulated to all schools" **Bob Lomas**. "Helmut Kohl's outburst appears to confirm your prophesy in your book Treason at Maastricht" **Walter Winwood, Australia**. "I admire not only the legal abilities you bring to bear but also your courage and patriotism" **Ray Hampton**. "I find it disturbing that Treason at Maastricht has not received wider publicity, it most certainly deserves it." **Christopher Gledhill, Switzerland**. "To me your book added another view of Maastricht which I can use against the European Union and for a sovereign Sweden." **Lars-Gunnar Liljestrand**. "Seldom have I read a book so well reasoned and I was intrigued to read its revelations about the Bilderbergers" **Professor Edward Duck, Germany**. "I congratulate you on the excellence of Treason at Maastricht" **Dr Peter Frankel**. "Thank you for writing Treason at Maastricht, it is brilliant." **Mrs M. Radcliffe.** "I am grateful to you for your willingness to research and codify such historic information - your fellow citizens I am sure are indebted to you for the strength of character you are showing by this work" **Barbara Rhett, USA.** "I must write in praise of Treason at Maastricht - I always wondered what it all meant - now I know" **Mrs K. Copeland**. "I am recommending Treason at Maastricht which I believe to be the most important book produced since the last war." **Barrie Linklater.**

THE FAILURE OF THE STATE

Essays on the Democratic Costs of Government

ISBN 0 9509353 3 6 Paperback 1989 Price £4.00

The author shows that, under all political parties, politics has become increasingly divorced from the people and Government increasingly irrelevant to Democracy. "The real burden on Society is not this Government but government per se." Occasional political elections, claims Atkinson, serve only to change the political horses while "the unresponsive carriage of the State continues on its way."

In a series of case studies the author shows that Conservative Government approve of Socialism and State power - so long as they and not Socialists are manipulating the levers of State control. "Corporatism is the Conservative's vice."

Atkinson warns that Corporatism, a combination of corporate power, interest group influence and State manipulation, was a cause of both the 1929 and 1987 stock market crashes and that another crash is probable unless institutional power is checked and individual responsibility increased. He warns of a slide into the kind of corporatism which "characterised Hitler's Germany and Mussolini's Italy," and claims that because the universal power of the State has grown Democracy is not so much secured as threatened by political elections, for "it is through the ballot box that the individual's freedom of action is converted into the State's universal control." The book shows for example how:

- Governments destroy the economic language which the people need to communicate with each other democratically; how the economic pronouncements of "international statesmanship" bring about the very instability which Governments try to avoid;

- State education in Britain has brought about literacy levels equivalent to those in the workhouses of the 1840's;
- The State was at the root of the environmental pollution from which it claimed to be protecting the people;
- The poorest people in Britain are subsidising the world's richest corporations;
- The State's "transitional" subsidies to the poorer regions have so far lasted 55 years;
- The "compassionate" State has brought about massive inequalities.

"Rodney Atkinson's latest box of intellectual fireworks offers repeated and persuasive evidence for his central verdict that the real burden on society is not this Government but government per se."

Lord Harris of High Cross, Institute of Economic Affairs.

"As politicians on the right step back to admire their handiwork Rodney Atkinson protests that their task has hardly begun. Closely and cleverly reasoned."

Matthew Parris of The Times

THE EMANCIPATED SOCIETY

ISBN 0 9509353 2 8 Hardback 1988 £10.00

The author rejects the traditional conflict between Right/Capitalism and Left/Socialism and contrasts instead Emancipated and Dependent Societies. The former are based on individual freedom, competition, overt social signals and continuous "social challenge" to authority. The latter are based on collectivism, State control, covert agreements and subservience to authority. Left/Right "horizontal politics" is rejected in favour of the Authoritarian/Libertarian "vertical axis" of political choice. No one, says the author, not even Government "can be permitted to decide the terms according to which they will be deemed successful." The role of the State must be based on the consent of the subordinated, limited to those activities which only the State can perform and capable of reduction or expansion according to public choice.

Atkinson describes a direct link between increasing State control and collectivism and ever more violent forms of individual "deviation" from social norms. He contrasts Government taxation with competition - a more democratic and less distorting form of "tax," and describes legitimate (emancipating) and illegitimate (controlling) Government activities as well as criteria for Government withdrawal.

State power leads to static definitions of justice, wealth, etc., while the more directly democratic public choice can more justly accommodate change. The book provides a wealth of new concepts to characterise the relationship between the State and the individual: the wrong consensus, just process, taxploitation, the dialectic of freedom, deviant energy, captive logic, circles of responsibility, social challenge and the critical distinction between emancipated and dependent societies.

"A powerful argument that is economically literate, historically erudite and philosophically cogent. Its central distinction between emancipated and dependent societies ought to acquire a much more central role in political thought and discourse."

Dr John Gray, Jesus College, Oxford.

"An illuminating beam of light and thought over the present confused landscape of political ideas."

Rt. Hon. David Howell, MP.

"A brilliant polemic. Atkinson's celebration of the virtues of free exchange and spontaneous process has shattered many collectivist illusions."

Professor Norman Barry, University of Buckingham.

"A refreshing and unique defense of liberty ... some first rate new approaches to property rights ... his case studies of government failures are fascinating."

Laissez Faire Books, New York.

"An argument for the moral superiority of the free market taken further and deeper than I have heard it developed before. An analysis of a high order of clarity and rigour: a powerful contribution."

Crossbow, Journal of the Conservative Bow Group